CYBER SECURITY AND HUMAN FACTORS

KEEPING INFORMATION SAFE

TARNVEER SINGH

This book is dedicated to my seven year old daughter whose love and curiosity inspired me to write this book. The next generation deserves better and this book intends to spark discussion on how we can improvo oybor socurity and safety.

CONTENTS

SECTION 1:

CYBERSECURITY: GETTING THE FUNDAMENTALS RIGHT

Introduction	2
What Impact Could Cyber Threats Have?	7
Cyber Crime	11
Cyber Safety	16
What Is Stopping Us?	27

SECTION 2:

CYBER VULNERABILITIES 29

Cyber Fundamentals	30
Technical Vulnerabilities	34
Physical And Environmental Vulnerabilities	35
People Vulnerabilities	37
Poor Governance Vulnerabilities	53

SECTION 3:

CYBER ATTACK VECTORS 58

Understand Your Attackers	59
Motivations, Means & Methodology	63

SECTION 4:

SECURITY IMPROVEMENT 72

Infosec Leadership	73
Risk Management	75
Business Continuity Management	83
Information Security Management – Individuals/SME	89
Information Security Management – Large Organisations	101
Information Management	113
Security Education, Awareness And Training	118
Human Factors	124

SECTION 1:

CYBERSECURITY: GETTING THE FUNDAMENTALS RIGHT

Introduction

In recent years, it has been clear that many services and applications are utterly unsecured, and that they can often leak our personal information, location, and credentials, whether by accident or deliberately.

This has caused a paradigm shift in the crime. Bank robbers used to solely rob banks because that's where the money was. While this may still be true, stealing money from a computer on the other side of the world is far less perilous than breaking into a bank or holding up employees with a shotgun. It can also be a lot more profitable, as we'll learn later in this book.

We are concerned about our privacy, yet we are willing to disclose our home address, email address, and credit card information to a company we have never heard of in exchange for a discount. We're lucky most of the time: the company turns out to be legitimate, and we get exactly what we paid for. However, we may not always be so fortunate - the offer may be a ruse, or the company's records may have been stolen, including the personal information we have provided, and now an unknown third party has it, which they can exploit, mistreat, or sell.

We feel threatened when we hear about new legislation that appears to give the police and security services an unrestricted right to snoop into our private lives. But we also feel encouraged when we hear that the security services have used the same legislation to intercept terrorist communications and prevent an attack. We understand that such surveillance is necessary, but we don't want it to apply to us because we haven't done anything illegal.

Cybercrime is becoming significantly more common than traditional burglary for the majority of individuals. When we buy things online, especially software for our smartphones and computers, we have to agree the seller's terms and conditions, but do we ever read them before clicking 'Agree'?

We expect that terms and conditions will be fair and meet with legal and reasonable trade standards, but they are frequently so long and written in legalese that we quickly lose interest in reading them. Of course, if you don't click 'Agree,' you won't be able to utilise the facility or software or at least only a limited version of it. We download 'apps' for our smartphones and tablet computers to make our lives easier, but many of them use the device's location whether we want them to or not, and this information can be collected, aggregated, and sold to others.

So, when things go wrong, we must bear at least some of the guilt - after all, we have given away information that may be used to identify us, as well as the opportunity for someone else to profit at our expense, whether intentionally or innocently.

The issue, however, is much larger than our individual shortcomings. Attackers will try to obtain information about us through using insecure applications and web-based services, and in this situation, the organisation that hosts the service and stores the information, rather than the consumer, is responsible.

While most organisations that are hacked remedy the problem (closing the stable door after the horse has bolted), some amend their terms and conditions to put the onus back on the customer in the event that their website has vulnerabilities.

Failure to secure our computers, smartphones, and tablets, as well as willingly handing up our credentials to strangers, is the digital equivalent of leaving the house unlocked and the keys in the car on the driveway when we leave on vacation.

There are so many data sources that listing them all would be impossible, but let's look at a few that might have an impact on our daily life in the context of cyber security. Our mobile phones capture call data records that detail who we phoned, when, from where, and for how long. Facebook, Twitter, and LinkedIn are just a few of the social media sites that gather text and photos. Location data from mobile phones and images we've shared can be recovered using the Global Positioning System (GPS). Data is collected through the usage of travel cards on buses and trains. Running shoes and body sensors provide data for fitness tracking. Data from congestion charge cameras, as well as data from number plate recognition, is collected. Credit and debit card transactions reveal a wealth of information about our personal habits. Personal information about us is contained in PayPal transactions and withdrawals from automated teller machines (ATMs). Passenger name records and loyalty cards on airlines contribute to data collection on our vacation habits, as well as information about us and our location. Because company ID cards were utilised for physical access control, data about us personally and our location was acquired throughout the working day. Our internet browsing history is connected to the MAC addresses and IP addresses of our computer devices. Bluetooth and wireless network (Wi-Fi) identifiers can be used to identify devices in a variety of ways. Passport scanners collect very personal data. Store loyalty cards allow us to track our purchasing patterns and see exactly what we buy on a regular basis. Access to our accounts and a plethora of sensitive information on us and our employers is controlled by user identifying names and passwords.

We could go on and on but consider this: if someone had access to all or even a significant portion of this data, they would know a lot about you, your movements, your business and personal relationships, your spending habits, your religion, sexual orientation and/or gender, political views, and your general health.

They might also expand their knowledge base by comparing some of your data to that of others, such as your Facebook acquaintances. This information is valuable not only to you, but also to others who might want to exploit it for lawful or illegal purposes. When we sign up for a "free" service, we are not getting anything for our money. We are exchanging some of our personal information for that service, and once we have handed it away, we no longer have control over it.

There are several basic words that should be grasped when discussing information security (including cyber security needs). The information security triangle — confidentiality, integrity, and availability – is a good place to start. However, there are two other terms that are currently considered to be equally important: authentication and non-repudiation.

Confidentiality refers to making sure that information is not revealed or made available to people who aren't supposed to have it. Loss of secrecy can be viewed as a goal in and of itself, such as the formula for a new drug, or as a means to an end, such as a password or PIN that grants access to a bank account. In either situation, a breach of confidentiality can have a significant impact on the individual or organisation that is the victim of a cyber-attack.

Integrity is concerned with the accuracy of data, regardless of how it is kept or communicated. Integrity entails ensuring that only authorised persons can produce, edit, or delete data, and it's strongly tied to confidentiality because it's usually those with unauthorised access to data who cause integrity problems.

Unauthorized changes to a student's grades from a 'fail' to a 'pass,' or unauthorised changes to a user's access level from 'guest' to 'administrator,' changing a criminal sentence from a custodial sentence to a fine, altering a mortgage applicant's credit rating, or removing details of previous illness from someone's medical records are all examples of integrity failures.

Availability refers to the ability of systems and the information stored on them to be accessed when and by whatever means are agreed upon. Customers of a bank, for example, would fairly expect to be able to access their accounts at any time of day or night, whether through online or telephone banking. Failures of availability almost always cause inconvenience, such as banking system failures which leave customers without access to their accounts and prevent inter-bank transfers. However, in extreme cases such as access to a hospital database containing details of an unconscious patient's allergies, they can be lifesaving.

Although the first three characteristics (availability, integrity, and confidentiality) have long been considered the "triad" of information security, the two next factors (authentication and non-repudiation) are also strong competitors.

Authentication is critical because it allows a system to confidently identify users. The traditional username and password have long been thought to be insufficient for making a positive identification, so additional methods have been introduced, one of which is 'two-factor' authentication, in which the traditional username and password (something you know) are supplemented by another form of identification, such as a token or smartphone app that generates a time-dependent one-time random number (something you have), or a biometric factor such as a fingerprint or iris scan (something you are).

Non-repudiation is equally important. In the event of a breach of confidentiality, integrity, or availability, even if someone has approved access to a system or information, they can deny taking the action that caused the problem. Non-repudiation is the process of ensuring that properly authenticated users cannot deny performing a specific action. This generally means that a detailed audit record of every activity taken by the user is retained.

Security is a phrase that encompasses both confidentiality and integrity, as well as availability to a lesser extent. It merely means that anything is safe from illegal access or harm, but the concept doesn't go any further.

When we, or our property, is protected from unwelcome intrusion, whether through the use of physical locks or a fully electronic device that prevents admission to those who do not have the correct keys, we feel safe. Security isn't just a technical or physical condition; it's also an emotional state of mind.

Privacy on the other hand, has a slightly different connotation. While the same principles apply as with security, privacy takes a more personal approach in that the subject matter, rather than being broad in reach, is much more personal to us. For example, someone living under a repressive government may regard the privacy of their political ideas greatly.

On the surface, security and privacy appear to be very similar, and in some cases, they are. However, there is a conflict between the two: for example, we rely on the government to keep us safe, both individually and as a nation, but we may believe that in order to do so, they have intruded on our privacy by intercepting our internet transactions and emails. It is possible that security will come at a cost.

Trust is the firm belief in the reliability, truth or ability of someone or something. It's very easy to lose trust, and it's very impossible to regain it. We put our faith in people, organisations, and systems without always thinking about or considering the implications. When trust is destroyed, the party responsible may suffer irreparable reputational or financial harm, such as when an online trader 'loses' our credit card information along with the information of thousands of other consumers. On rare occasions, however, the stock price returns to normal or near-normal levels.

Big data and data mining encompasses not just vast amounts of data, but also many data sources and their consolidation, as well as the skill and desire to sift through records and identify patterns, thereby transforming data into knowledge. For example, consider a large ecommerce website: its databases may contain the registration and payment information for millions of customers; tens of thousands of items; the combination of which consumers have purchased which things; and when, when, how much they paid, and how they paid. The ecommerce website's capacity to make solid business decisions with that data is enormous, but only that skill will decide its ultimate value to both the ecommerce website and the consumer.

The process of acquiring massive data is referred to as data aggregation. Some large data (like in the example above) comes from a single source, while other applications will necessitate the inclusion of multiple data sets. These can be obtained directly by the organisation that requires the data, or they can be brought in from outside if they are not available within the organisation. Data aggregation may be a very powerful method for integrating seemingly unrelated data sets into one that can be utilised to create a complete profile of a subject if done correctly. Data aggregation, on the other hand, is much more than a way of getting massive data. Combining poor classification data sources, for example, can result in a gold mine of personally identifiable information, posing a whole new set of security concerns (PII).

Cyber security is intertwined with a number of different types of security. It overlaps with information security, which is concerned with the protection of confidentiality, integrity, and availability of information in all areas, not only cyberspace. It also has some overlap with application security, which is focused with introducing controls and measurements to an organization's applications, whether software, hardware, or data. It is similar to network security, which is concerned with assuring the security of an organization's networks, both within and between organisations, as well as between the organisation and its users. Server operating systems (OS) and, increasingly, the virtualization layer and accompanying management tools are all part of network security. Furthermore, cybersecurity intersects with Internet security, which is concerned with preserving an organization's internet-based services' availability and reliability, as well as protecting individual users at work and at home. It also overlaps with critical information infrastructure protection, which includes the cyber security aspects of critical information infrastructure (CII) elements of a country.

What Impact Could Cyber Threats Have?

Cyber impacts or consequences are the result of an unintended incident, such as when a threat exploits a vulnerability. Impacts come in a variety of shapes and sizes, but they all necessitate some sort of decision. Some affects can be accepted because they are minor, but many cannot and must be mitigated or eliminated through some type of countermeasure, control, or treatment. Many of the consequences will be felt on a personal or individual basis, while others will have a far broader impact on businesses.

Individuals in the home or in small businesses, as well as those working in major corporations, are affected by personal impacts. The loss or disclosure of personal information is one of the most concerning consequences for individuals. This might be nearly anything about our personal or professional lives that we'd rather keep secret, but which, for whatever reason, would become awkward or embarrassing if made public. It's remarkable how much information you can gather about someone without ever having heard of them or knowing that they are aware of the situation. There are a lot of people with the same name, and they all seem to have the same email address. Many of us get emails addressed to others on a regular basis. It is easy to build up a blurry picture of them over time, completely accidentally. We know their names, their occupations, where they reside (approximately and in a few cases, exactly), their interests, and some of their buying patterns. I'm sure I could learn a lot more if I set my mind to it, but the more essential point is that they are either completely unaware of this or absolutely indifferent that much of their personal information has wound up in the hands of someone for whom it was never meant. This is due to one simple fact: they wrote their email address wrong, or the person who sent them an email did. We gladly sign up for social media sites and provide information about ourselves. Facebook, Twitter, and LinkedIn are just three examples of social media platforms where a wealth of information about us may be uncovered, including our prior schooling, university experience, work history, interests and hobbies, family life, and much more. Individuals aren't the only ones who can generate issues for themselves. Consider the instance of a CEO who was meeting with the CEO of another company on a regular basis in order to discuss a merger. His teenage daughter shared a photo of the place they visited, along with a message about her father being in a meeting at a particular company, on one occasion when he had his family with him. Someone who followed her on social media put two and two together and made a few phone calls, resulting in the fact that a highly sensitive debate became public information, impacting the firms' share prices and effectively sabotaging the project.

Credentials of individuals are major business. Bank and credit card account information, usernames, email addresses, passwords, and other personal information are bought and sold on the internet for surprisingly low prices. An attacker who can obtain these in quantity can profit from the information in a number of ways, including using the credentials himself to carry out attacks against the individuals in question, or selling them in bulk to others who are better suited to carry out the assaults. Depending on the sort of credentials revealed, the consequences on the individual can be significant. If the victim is fortunate, they may be able to detect the attack early on and only lose a modest amount of money. It can be considerably more catastrophic if they are unfortunate.

Money is a primary motive for cyber-attackers, thus if the opportunity arises, they will strive to steal as much as they can. In some cases, where the individual can demonstrate that they have done their due diligence and protected their computer and bank cards as best they can, the finance organisation will accept responsibility for the losses; however, where individuals have been careless or negligent, they risk losing significant sums of money. If, for example, a loss empties one's bank account right before to a direct debit being taken for a mortgage payment, and this is then indicated against the individual's credit rating, the individual's financial standing or credit worthiness may be impacted.

Personal reputations can readily be ruined by cyber-attacks. Consider someone whose email account has been hacked or whose account username has been used by an attacker. It is relatively easy to send out harmful emails that might ruin their reputation overnight. More often than not, especially if the recipients know the person well, they accept that the account has been abused, but the consequences of receiving hostile communications from someone you don't know can be far more serious. Reputation and trust go hand in hand. People with a good reputation are more trustworthy, and vice versa, and losing trust in someone means that their word is no longer trustworthy.

Theft of intellectual property is closely tied to the theft of money, because even if no money is taken, the IP owner's ability to generate money through sales is taken away. An attacker stealing the original material and claiming it as their own is a secondary and far more serious loss of IP, putting the original IP owner at a severe disadvantage.

Identity theft is widespread among persons who are targeted by organised groups that use that person's email address to send hate mail to everyone on their contact list, steal money from their bank account, rack up credit card bills, and nearly destroy their personal and professional lives. While the culprits could be identified, they would never be prosecuted because they would be beyond the security services' authority.

Because an attacker may betray their identity if they carry out too many actions using the stolen identity, identity theft is frequently linked to cyber theft, but in the event of a quick 'smash and grab,' the attacker can discard the identity as soon as they have the money.

Organisational impacts Include many of the above. The overall impacts, however, could be substantially bigger due to the scale of organisations, both in terms of the number of people involved and the amount of money involved. These might easily include a company's partial or complete demise, as well as significant job losses.

When a cyber-attack is successful, the organization's brand and reputation are usually harmed, especially if it becomes evident that the organisation did not take any precautions either to prevent the assault from occurring in the first place or to successfully deal with it once it has occurred. It's sometimes because one or both of these have resulted in the loss of intellectual property or customer data. Customers may lose trust in organisations that have suffered such an impact and opt not to do business with them in the future.

The financial impacts on a company's revenue streams might be disastrous. Customers will be unable to place orders as a result of cyber-attacks, and an organisation will be unable to trade online. This will not only result in immediate revenue loss, but it will also frequently result in downstream losses when clients move their company elsewhere.

Following a successful cyber-attack that damages the company's brand, the stock price is likely to plummet. A decrease in share value is a common occurrence under normal conditions and would not be cause for alarm, but in these unique circumstances, it could take months or years for an organisation to recover its share price.

Furthermore, cyber-attacks might prevent an organisation from ordering items from suppliers, paying them for things already received, or paying employees' wages or salaries. Organizations can be penalised for mishandling client data in some instances, notably in highly regulated industries, especially if their acts violate data protection legislation. They may also incur further financial losses as a result of interest charges for late payments, particularly to Her Majesty's Revenue and Customs (HMRC) for late corporate tax payments.

In addition to any revenue losses, businesses will incur expenditures in repairing damage caused by a successful cyber-attack, which may entail the implementation of corrective information security policies. There's a chance that a company may be targeted by ransomware and will be forced to pay a ransom to get their data back. The alternative would be for the company to spend a lot of time and money trying to recover all of its compromised systems. The cost of such a recovery process could in some situations far outweigh the ransom demanded.

When an organization's operational systems, such as development systems, production control systems, stock control systems, and the like, are harmed by a cyber-attack, operational failures can ensue. The consequences could be disastrous, as the organisation may be unable to function for the duration of the situation.

Most, if not all, of these failures will undoubtedly have financial consequences, since the organization's ability to offer products or services to its consumers will result in revenue loss, as well as possible brand and reputation harm.

The failure of a software upgrade at the Royal Bank of Scotland a few years ago resulted in 6.5 million clients being unable to access their online accounts, receive incoming payments, or make transfers to other RBS or other bank accounts. Various regulatory organisations fined the bank a total of £56 million. While this isn't a specific cyber security event, it does show what can happen when system upgrades aren't thoroughly verified before being deployed.

Employees who are forced to be laid off as a result of financial losses or operational failures, or who choose to quit because they have lost faith in the organization's capacity to appropriately plan for and respond to cyber security disruptions, can have a significant influence on people. These personnel losses result in a significant loss of expertise.

Cyber Crime

Cybercrime can be avoided with the effective use of information security. Cybercrime definitions are riddled with flaws. Many cybercrimes look like 'normal' crimes, but they always have a cyber component to them - either as a means to an end, including cyber systems or networks, or as both a means and a target, involving cyber systems or networks. Anyone can be a victim of cybercrime, whether or not they are online. Even if you have never used a computer, a criminal can spend your money once they get your bank or credit card information.

Cybercrime can encompass but in no way restricted to:

- **Cyber-trespass:** Like its pre-digital cousin, this category combines together cyber-offenses that include 'crossing or violating borders,' however these are digital rather than physical barriers. For example, the cyber-trespass category could include offences like hacking or unauthorised data access.

- **Cyber-deception and theft :** This category includes crimes like online fraud and IP theft, which are typically addressed separately.

- **Cyber-porn and obscenity:** In addition to the well-known range of child pornography-related offences, Wall's category included other sorts of online sexual behaviours that are generally frowned upon but not criminalised, such as the distribution of pornography.

- **Cyber-violence.** This encompasses the types of emotional violence that can be perpetrated online, such as bullying and harassment. However, there is also mention of more extreme acts, such as cyberterrorism.

Illegal interception, data interference, system interference, and device misuse are all examples of crimes against the confidentiality, integrity, and availability of computer data and systems. Forgery, fraud, and other computer-related offences are examples. Child pornography and terrorist materials are two examples of content-related offences. There are copyright and associated rights-related offences. There are additional secondary liabilities, such as unauthorised access.

Financial theft, on the other hand, is the most common sort of cybercrime. Unlike a traditional bank robbery, when physical currency is stolen, this form of crime poses little or no risk to the criminal, as there are no firearms, masks, or getaway cars, and it can result in a far larger payoff.

One disadvantage of cyber-based financial theft is that there may be an audit trail identifying where the money came from and where it was transferred to. Money laundering and utilising middlemen to distance themselves from the criminal conduct have been used by cyber criminals to remedy this flaw in their scheme.

Cyber criminals are increasingly less interested in obtaining individual personal details in order to commit crimes, not that we should be complacent about this, but instead are looking for details of thousands or millions of individuals' personal details in order to maximise their return on investment, because each piece of information has a value.

They frequently accomplish this by selling the information to larger criminal gangs, whose resources enable them to utilise the information in large-scale spam campaigns, such as those purporting to sell high-end watches and mobile phones.

Alternatively, criminal gangs target specific groups of people by offering non-existent vehicles for sale on legal websites. After agreeing to purchase the vehicle via email with the fraudsters, buyers receive an email pretending to be from Amazon indicating that their money would be kept in an escrow account until the buyer confirms that they agree with the arrangement, thereby providing 'buyer protection.' Of course, after the buyer has deposited the funds to the 'escrow account,' the transaction is complete, and the vehicle is no longer visible.

The term 'hacker' originally referred to someone who was curious about how things functioned, dismantled them to learn more about them, and then reassembled them in a way that improved their performance. A hacker was eventually defined as someone who built software that performed a beneficial activity in a graceful manner. A piece of code that was condensed to run in a relatively small memory space was deemed a "wonderful hack" when computer memory was an extremely expensive commodity.

Some of the greatest inventions have come from this benign activity, but unfortunately, the term 'hacking' has been tarnished by the media in recent years, referring to those with less honourable intentions who break into other people's computers for fun, revenge, or to make a statement of some kind – often on political, ethical, or environmental issues, and some hackers will simply deface a website (usually its 'landing' page) in order to make a statement of some kind – often

Some hackers merely break into a system "because it exists" and "because they can." This serves no use other than to show their friends how brilliant they are and how vulnerable the target's security is. This intrusion, known as 'planting the flag,' is intended to demonstrate their achievement and, hopefully, garner them the respect of their colleagues.

This type of hacking can be quite benign at times, yet it can result in the defacement of internet pages. This type of hacker is often referred to as a "script kiddie," who takes advantage of software and techniques they've discovered in the darkest corners of the internet, and while they may mean no harm, serious damage can easily occur due to their limited knowledge and ability to use the software and tools. Script kids, on the other hand, can evolve into full-fledged cyber criminals if they are encouraged and given the opportunity to do so, and this can result in significant damage.

Many organisations affected by this type of hacking admit to being careless with their cyber security and respond by tightening their security practises, while others, as in the case of George McKinnon, who was accused of hacking into NASA and US military computers, may press for arrest, prosecution, and even deportation.

Exploitation elevates intrusion to a whole new level. A hacker who exploits a system they've broken into may exfiltrate, erase, or distort data, which can have disastrous consequences not only for the target organisation, but also for its customers and system users.

Denial of service (DoS) attacks are commonly used to prohibit genuine users from accessing a company's website, while they can be used for other purposes. The reasons for this will vary – some will be used as a form of blackmail (pay us money, and we'll stop); others will be motivated by political or other activism (commonly referred to as hacktivism) and will aim to cause financial loss and/ or public embarrassment; and still others will be in retaliation for some real or perceived action.

Some DoS attacks are aimed to crash a website by overloading it to the point where it can no longer function, while others merely block lawful access, preventing the supporting apps from receiving and processing service requests. In either case, the website's response will be significantly slowed and, in most cases, totally halted. DoS attacks can also be directed at an organization's email service, such as by a disgruntled employee, causing the Exchange server to become overburdened and stop handling valid email traffic.

The distributed (DDoS) attacks are the most common types of DoS attacks nowadays, in which numerous computers cooperate together to overload the target website. Because very few stand-alone systems are capable of successful attacks against very big websites, attackers usually employ botnets to assemble sufficient capability.

Copyright infringement is a big business, although it usually only pays out in the form of 'free' items for the recipient. Music, films, books, photos, and computer software are all examples of copyright infringement. While the copyright holder usually retains ownership of the item, illicit copies are made, depriving the owner of the profit they may have had from it.

Copyrighted material is frequently transmitted through file-sharing websites like The Pirate Bay, which use so-called "torrent" files to direct consumers back to the specific file or files to be downloaded. The downloaded material is shared amongst users as more people join the sharing process, and dissemination is peer-to-peer.

Because many copies were produced in such a short period of time, it is also impossible to identify the person who originally hosted the information. While torrenting files is not illegal, the content may be, especially if it is protected by copyright and the owner has not consented to it being shared in this manner. The annual losses to numerous industries are estimated to be in the billions of dollars.

While intellectual property theft is comparable in many ways, the sale or dissemination of the stolen property is usually not. Unlike copyright infringement, which allows a large audience to benefit from free software, music, or video material, IP theft is more commonly done to order for one or a few select customers, and rarely becomes widely spread. Previously, this would have been referred regarded as 'industrial espionage.'

The financial loss to the owner, on the other hand, can be enormous, especially when a pharmaceutical company develops a ground-breaking treatment only to lose its formula to a competitor who can then sell it for less than the cost of production, packaging, marketing, and distribution.

While the employment of so-called dark patterns isn't illegal, it does tend to blur the line between fairness and dishonesty. When you visit a website, you may discover that, due to imprecise writing on web pages, you have consented to download software or accepted an offer that you did not mean to accept. Web page designers often purposefully place selection boxes in strange places or make the options difficult so that you are compelled to make their choice rather than your own.

There are entire industries dedicated to determining the shapes, sizes, and colours of buttons, click boxes, and text that users are most likely to click on – and those that they are least likely to click on – while visiting a website. The data is sold to companies that are creating new websites or updating existing ones, with the goal of enticing consumers to choose the company's option rather than their own.

In extreme circumstances, products you didn't request may be added to your online shopping cart, and if you're not careful, you can end up buying something you don't want as well as the items you want.

Dark patterning is the act of making web sites perplexing, and the techniques are incredibly subtle, based on established features of human behaviour. If you are trying to book a flight, for example, you may notice that the airline or travel agency offers to sell you travel insurance, and unless you choose to opt out rather than in, you may discover that you have purchased it and may have problems getting a refund.

These black patterns aren't strictly forbidden, but they represent sharp practise in the imaginations of many individuals. Although pressure groups are forming to combat this by establishing a code of conduct for web developers, it is possible that only legislation will fully resolve the issue, as the offending organisations' sales and marketing policies are likely to drive the practise for the foreseeable future, especially where it increases revenue.

Cyber Safety

The act of harassing or bullying an individual or group of people via cyber-based technologies such as social media, text messaging, and the like is known as cyber harassment or cyberbullying. I chose to separate this from cybercrime since some components of cyberbullying are not technically criminal or civil offences, yet they are a huge problem in today's society. Some jurisdictions, however, have enacted legislation that expands the definition of harassment to include internet harassment. The distinction between online harassment and cyber bullying is that with internet harassment, anyone or any organisation can be a victim, whereas with cyber bullying, the victims are primarily children.

Cyber harassment or bullying can start in the same way that traditional harassment or bullying does, with a nasty comment about another person that offends them. The bully (who may or may not be a control freak) seizes on this effect and exploits it again and again, often urging others to join in. The consequences can be severe, and some people who have been harassed or bullied for a long time have been forced to commit suicide. Cyber bullying or harassment is just as aggressive and deadly, and it can come in a variety of forms.

Cybercriminologists have spent a lot of time looking for online behaviours that influence the chance of committing a crime or being a victim. While some of these criteria have remained important as technology has progressed, others have become less so in terms of identifying cybervictimization. Before getting into specific behaviours, it's important emphasising that many academics continue to emphasise the link between growing online presence and criminality simply as a matter of opportunity. To put it another way, as one's online profile grows, so does the chance of being a victim of or perpetrator of cyberbullying. Scholars have discovered numerous harmful online behaviours that influence the probability of cyberbullying perpetration and/or victimisation. Given the nature of cybercrime, the most problematic activities reported across the literature are those that place persons in close contact to others, which makes intuitive sense. Many studies have discovered that children who use chatrooms, instant messaging, and social media sites are more likely to be victims of and perpetrators of cyberbullying. Furthermore, numerous studies have shown that those who participate in risky behaviour that displays vulnerability are more likely to be subjected to cyberbullying. Bypassing security systems, uploading risqué photographs, or victimising others, for example, raises the danger of being subjected to cyberbullying.

Given the well-documented dangers of social networking sites, researchers have concentrated their efforts on determining which behaviours on these platforms influence the likelihood of perpetrating or being the victim of cyberbullying. Although this field of study is still in its early stages, scientists have discovered that having a large number of friends, engaging in negative content (directly or through friends), making status updates, and using private messaging all raise the likelihood of being subjected to cyberbullying. Despite the importance of this online behaviour, researchers have focused on determining whether particular offline behaviours influence the probability of experiencing or perpetrating cyberbullying. Cyberbullies may, predictably, exhibit clinically abnormal levels of disobedience and use addictive substances. Cybervictims, on the other hand, may be more likely to suffer from despair and other harmful repercussions.

Cyber harassment is intended to alert the victim to the possibility of something specific happening to them. Threats can be made by people who are known to the victim or by people who are unknown to the victim, and targets can be broadened to include organisations that the person issuing the threats believes have wronged them or someone else.

Sending threatening and unwanted communications over omnipresent platforms (i.e., email, instant messaging, social media), as well as leveraging publicly available online information for criminal objectives, all fall under the definition of cyber stalking. Cyber stalkers operate in two modes. First, they can watch their victim's movements and activities invisibly, without alerting them to the fact that they are being followed. Second, they can still track their victim's movements and activities, but this time more openly, with the victim being aware that they are being followed, but usually unaware of the stalker's identity. The victim may be someone the stalker is familiar with, such as a relative, former partner, or neighbour; nevertheless, the victim may be someone the stalker is unfamiliar with, such as a celebrity, an organization's CEO, or a politician. Cyber stalking's main goal is usually to create distress to the person who is the target, and it is commonly successful. In certain cases, cyber stalking involves instilling fear in the victim by informing them that the stalker is watching them, but this is usually where it ends.

Cyber trolling is a type of verbal abuse intended to intimidate or offend the target. Cyber trolls engage in confrontational or unpleasant online behaviour and, unlike cyber stalkers, make little effort to conceal their identity. Online trolling is also distinct from cyber bullying or harassment in that it is done openly, maybe in the hopes of gaining support for the cyber troll's point of view and is intended to cause the victim anguish. Cyber trolling also varies from free and intelligent debate in that it does not allow or encourage a rational exchange of ideas, instead focusing solely on the cyber troll's negative, often strongly voiced, and generally irrational viewpoints.

Cyber trolls will frequently post inflammatorily comments on social media or online discussion forums in order to elicit a reaction or response from the victim, which will invariably provide the troll with more opportunities to post comments, and this can quickly escalate into a full-fledged online brawl. According to conventional opinion, the best method to deal with cyber trolls is to ignore their comments, as their actions will quickly fade if there is no reaction, response, or interaction. Alternatively, offending people can be disabled on many discussion boards, preventing victims of trolling from seeing their comments. Trolls can be reported to the forum moderator, and their accounts may be terminated as a result.

Cyber warfare is the process by which one nation state or politically motivated group attacks another's critical infrastructure (CI), political process, or even offensive or defensive military capacity. Warfare was, until recently, a rather simple process. One country state picked a conflict with another, and their two sets of armed forces went at it until one nation state capitulated and the war was done. Only when more country states joined in on either side did things get really difficult, but the end conclusion was typically the same. Because both 'sides' are usually evenly matched, this type of warfare is commonly referred to as symmetric warfare.

The growth of terrorism, on the other hand, blurred the lines. A militant group might declare war on a number of countries, often without regard for whether or not those countries shared the same religious or ideological beliefs. Because terrorist groups rarely have the same purchasing power as nation states, their weapons are frequently home-made such as improvised explosive devices (IEDs), for example, but because they can be used in unconventional ways – not just in battle – they are frequently deployed as roadside bombs or detonated by suicide bombers. Asymmetric warfare is named by the fact that one side may have a tiny number of soldiers compared to the other yet can still deliver devastating effects. A cyber-attack or cyber invasion by one nation state against another, on the other hand, does not necessarily imply that they are at war, and the attack could merely be viewed as an act of aggression rather than a formal declaration of war.

Because technology can be deployed by one nation state against another, or by small groups – even individuals – against a much bigger foe, cyber warfare employs both symmetric and asymmetric means. Unless the other side can find the attacker and instruct a drone to deliver lethal ordnance, cyber warfare can be performed just as readily from an armchair, a stool in a cybercafé, or an office chair in a government building, and carries few of the perils of traditional combat. If they work for the government or military, or if they are a highly skilled and experienced individual, a 'cyber warrior' can walk home safe in the knowledge that they are unlikely to be shot at after completing their daily or nightly shift, despite possibly causing their adversary significant cyber havoc.

The capacity to gather secret information without the owner's permission or knowledge is referred to as espionage. Governments often conduct surveillance on one another. They've been doing it for centuries and will undoubtedly continue to do so in the future. Sometimes espionage is about discovering what another country possesses – such as its nuclear missile capacity – while other times it is about discovering another government's objectives, which may be more difficult to detect but can be surmised given enough data.

Cyber espionage is no different, however unlike traditional espionage, which requires spies to put themselves in danger by working in enemy territory, cyber espionage may be carried out safely from the comfort of one's own office with no risk to the spy. If a field agent is apprehended and exposed as a spy for another country, the diplomatic fallout can last months or years. However, because nation-state cyber espionage departments take great pains to conceal their identities and frequently disguise attacks as coming from somewhere else, it is difficult, if not impossible, to prove who carried out an attack, and assumptions, even if correct, are insufficient evidence.

Surveillance differs from espionage in several ways, not in the way it is carried out, but in the goals and purposes it pursues. Surveillance focuses on keeping track of people's activities, communications, and contacts, and in terms of cyber warfare, it's more analogous to terrorist investigations. Because both security services and the military must work together to track down suspected terrorists, there is a particular overlap in the strategies utilised by the two. Surveillance has played a key role in identifying and locating individuals and groups with clear intentions to commit acts of terrorism, and while the details remain classified, the government has stated that careful surveillance has prevented a number of potentially lethal attacks, and they are using this argument to push for legislation that makes it easier for security services to monitor the activities of the general public.

Although governments and security services do not openly discuss this aspect of cyber warfare, infiltrating activist groups has proven to be one of the most effective (though risky) techniques of conventional surveillance, allowing operatives to identify potential targets and their leaders.

In terms of objectives, cyber infiltration is no different, and agents must be able to infiltrate online groups just as readily, and because they are physically separated from the rest of the group, they are considerably less at danger if their activities are discovered, and they are 'outed.'

For its teams of saboteurs, cyber sabotage is far less dangerous. They will identify and monitor their target from afar, then carefully position their weapon, which will subsequently destroy the enemy's infrastructure, using one of the attack methods we've already discussed. It has been demonstrated that sabotage of key infrastructure parts is conceivable. In 2007, the Idaho National Laboratory in the United States conducted a test in which it opened and reopened the circuit breakers connecting a 50 MW generator to the grid out of synchronisation, causing the generator to shatter. On a broader scale, the impact on a major power plant capable of generating hundreds of megawatts of electricity might have a significant economic impact on the country.

Only in terms of magnitude does psychological cyber warfare differ from cyber harassment or bullying. Psychological cyber warfare is carried out by much larger groups, such as terrorist organisations and country states, whereas cyber bullies are usually individuals or small groups. Psychological cyber warfare usually serves one of two purposes. First, it is employed by one organisation or government to demoralise the people of another country in order for them to withdraw their support for the present system. During World War II, both the Allies and the Axis forces used psychological warfare radio broadcasts to incite opposition to their respective regimes. Psychological cyber warfare merely shifts the medium from broadcast radio to the internet in this regard. The other goal is population enslavement and repression by the government – frequently an oppressive regime – which can utilise cyber tactics to prevent people from standing up to it and disseminate fear of the consequences of doing so. Not only do such regimes utilise the internet as a weapon in this way, but they also routinely restrict how the public uses the internet by blocking access to websites that do not favour or actively oppose the regime. Negative news reports about a dictatorship can be censored in the international press, and glowing portrayals of the regime's leadership and successes can be substituted — all while the people lacks the fundamental comforts enjoyed by less constrained cultures.

We are constantly under observation, whether we are aware of it or not. Cyber surveillance can be divided into two categories. The first that comes to mind is that of intrusive or invasive snooping, which is normally linked with security services monitoring, especially since the Snowden revelations. The second is the collecting and use of data about us by organisations with whom we engage on a regular basis, which appears to be far less intrusive on the surface.

The reason for targeted monitoring is because the subject has attracted the notice of the authorities, who are keenly interested in his or her behaviour. Normally (but not always), such persons are criminals or terrorists, and we are relieved to know that the proper police or security services are paying close attention to them. When we have the impression that we are being watched, we tend to take a different perspective, and it is here that we are aware of the problem that the police and security services face when they don't have a specific target in mind: they must collect far more data than they need, and then (in theory) discard the data that isn't relevant or that they don't need to keep. Because the cost of storage media is continuing to decline, data collection and storage are becoming less expensive over time, and as a result, businesses will collect and store as much data as they can and preserve it until they figure out how to best use it.

In the wake of the Snowden revelations, blanket surveillance is becoming the standard. Security services on both sides of the Atlantic are listening in on phone calls, emails, internet searches, and transactions without necessarily having the legal authority to do so, which is concerning because we have no control over it. The word 'collect' has a different meaning for the National Security Agency (NSA). We would think of this as just data monitoring, interception, and storage, but the National Security Agency (NSA) views it to also involve data analysis.

How much personal information do you willingly give up when you look for anything on the internet? There's probably a lot more than you realise. Let's consider the case of Amazon for a moment. They retain a detailed record of everything you've purchased from them, so if you need something similar again, you can order it with a few clicks and without having to remember who supplied it.

They also keep track of all the items you've recently searched for. They are aware of your interests and wish to sell you more. Your search request is saved when you use an online search engine. The links that you click on after that are saved. Every website you visit on a frequent basis is automatically saved as a 'favourite' by the search engine.

Most Western countries enable the communications company supplying the service to keep records of any website and messaging service visited by their people from any device. The data is then accessible to government departments. Apart from the greater violation of privacy, one of the main worries is that all it takes is one bad actor to gain access to the entire database.

Not alone does search create a digital trace; every time you visit a website, a little file known as a 'cookie' might be left on your computer. Many cookies are required for you to be able to use the website - for example, when you shop online, the retailer needs to be able to link your shopping basket to your computer so that you can purchase exactly what you want. Other cookies are less useful to you, and they may keep track of which pages you've visited, whose flights you've looked at, or which cameras you've looked at. These may not appear to be particularly bad things, but the next time you visit an airline ticket website, it may just utilise the information that you've been there before to raise the ticket price or inform you that the cheaper flight is sold out and you must choose a more costly flight. Surveillance and subsequent manipulation are a very subtle sort of surveillance that we are typically unaware of.

Other cookies keep track of these details so that advertisers can place ads in prominent locations on the screen. If you use one of the major search engines or shopping websites to research a specific type of camera, you will almost probably see an offer from one of the photographic providers when you return to the site. This is harmless in and of itself, but keep in mind that the search engine or website may have saved every single item you've looked for. Advertisers can use this information to create a highly accurate picture of you as a person, and (in principle) offer highly relevant advertising to you. The advertiser will, of course, be advertising what they want to sell you, not necessarily what you want to buy.

The majority of websites do not allow you to disable cookies. They usually give you the option of clicking 'I understand' or something similar, 'Tell me more,' or simply ignoring the notice. Many websites employ an 'implied consent' approach, which means that if you ignore the cookie notification and continue to use the website, you have implicitly given your permission for cookies to be placed.

When you send or receive an email, your provider's server automatically saves a copy in case you need it later. Email analysis, whether obtained through interception or access to an ISP's servers, can provide a surveillance organisation with a wealth of information, as there may be a complete archive of all emails sent and received in the 'conversation,' and each email sent and received will contain details of the sender and recipients.

Email can be just as dangerous as cookies on a website. Unless you erase every duplicate of every email you've written or received, including those you've forwarded to others, the message will live on in some form someplace, and emails, like online searches, can tell a lot about you.

Unless all emails including personal information are encrypted, they can be read like a postcard, duplicated, printed, forwarded to others, and used in evidence against you if they contain something negative you have said or that implicates you in a crime. In the area of cyber surveillance, email may be a very effective tool, because not only can the content provide vital information to security services and law enforcement agencies, but the 'to' and 'from' sections in an email can also provide additional surveillance targets.

Email, far from being a blessing, may be a curse, and many of us would question how and why we have amassed so much rubbish in our inboxes. Receiving spam via email might potentially invite cyber-attacks.

Many people have abandoned their traditional mobile phones. The quantity of data that can be taken from you thanks to smartphones is mind-boggling. The phrase "smartphone" is most likely an oxymoron. The device is actually a small computer that runs applications, takes photos, and also makes and receives phone calls and text messages, so it's not all that different from your laptop in that regard – just smaller and often no less powerful. Unless you turn off your phone, your network operator always has a rough idea of where you are and can route calls and texts to you. Unless you've gone into your smartphone's security settings, you'll almost certainly be recording your GPS coordinates, which will pinpoint your whereabouts to within a metre or two.

Every app on your smartphone that need your location to function can now track your movements. If you're using a mapping programme, this is ok, but if you're just playing a game, it's not. Of course, the app developer isn't interested in your location, but they might be selling your information, along with hundreds of others, to a third party.

Have you ever used your smartphone to capture a picture? The location was saved in the exif data, which is the metadata of a photograph. That exif data became available when you uploaded that photograph to the internet. The exif data will also include information on the date and location of the photograph, as well as the serial numbers of the camera and lens you used.

Individuals can be identified in real time using a contemporary camera or smartphone, or from a previously taken snapshot using facial recognition. The image is compared to others in a central database, and complex algorithms are employed to match features like the eyes, lips, and head shape, among others. Once a match has been made in this manner, more information on the person can be obtained, either from the same database or via a broader internet search. Although the police and security services must make extensive use of this in tracking down and monitoring suspected criminals and terrorists, we must face the fact that if someone's photograph is posted on the internet, they can be identified and possibly tracked regardless of whether or not they have committed a crime. However, if face recognition is used for authentication, it is easy to mislead the matching process by wearing a mask, therefore it should not be utilised alone. Consider someone who was photographed while participating in a nonviolent protest in a country where the government has complete control over its citizens. The demonstrator may then be visited by the secret police and disappear forever.

As we stated earlier in this book, terms and conditions can be a huge issue. We don't even look at them. Due to their length and confusing 'legalese' terminology, few people will have read them from beginning to end and will have simply clicked on the 'Accept' button, potentially relinquishing any control they may have had over their personal information. Of course, software sellers give us no choice - there is no discussion, and if we want the software, we must relinquish any rights we may have previously held. Furthermore, and maybe more concerning, by signing away our rights by accepting the terms and conditions, we may be exposing ourselves to surveillance, such as disclosing our location when using a smartphone.

When you initially use an app on your smartphone or tablet computer, you'll have to agree to the terms of service, which almost always include the ability for the app author's company to keep, use, and sell information about what you've done. Not only that, but because many of us don't turn off the GPS feature on our smartphones, the app may have the capacity to track your whereabouts and report it back to the provider — even when you aren't using it. Even if you read the terms and conditions when you first load a programme or make an online purchase, the seller may amend them at any time (their authority to do so without informing you may be embedded in the original terms and conditions), and you may never notice the changes.

Store loyalty programmes allow the store to keep track of everything we buy there, including how much we paid, where we bought it, and when we bought it. Store loyalty programmes are a fantastic invention. The deals that the store then offers us are usually good value for money, and they often help the store get rid of items that it wouldn't be able to sell otherwise. We may be eligible for a discount on certain items, free coffee and cake on our next visit, an invitation to a "special" pre-Christmas shopping event, or the opportunity to skip the line when a new product is released. Some stores now offer a smartphone app that allows you to access their website, your account, and a variety of other features. Have you ever received an email out of the blue from a company you'd never done business with before and wondered how you got it? It's very likely that you did so when you signed up for a loyalty programme. Many businesses use deceptive techniques to lead you to make the wrong decision when filling out such a form, and because you didn't read the terms and conditions, you may discover that you have agreed to the store selling your contact information to a third party. Of course, you can try to modify it, but it's usually too much trouble or the tools to do so are too tough to discover on the company's website, so you just accept it. Is this a problem with cyber security? Definitely, because a third party now has all of your information, as well as the information of the store that offered you the loyalty programme, and those details might end up anyplace if the third company's network is hacked.

Credit cards allow us to make impulsive purchases when we may not have enough dollars in our bank account; there is no financial charge if we pay off the outstanding balance on our credit cards each month; and they even operate as protection if something goes wrong when we make purchases. The same can be said about modern payment methods. mPay, ApplePay, AndroidPay, and travel money cards like Caxton all benefit both the provider and the consumer, but all come with the same level of risk. When you combine a credit or debit card with a reward programme, things start to look a lot better for the supplier. When you combine them with their smartphone app, which tracks your activities, you may find that the next time you go grocery shopping, you receive a text message when you pass a specific supermarket aisle offering you a special discount. Combine them even more where retailers provide the SIM card for your mobile phone (and thus know your regular contacts and movements), and you may have agreed to allow the retailer to include the fact that their banking service is aware of all your current account financial transactions if you accepted the terms and conditions.

Travel cards allow you to load money onto the card and use it whenever you want – on the subway, buses, the river, and even some over-ground train services. Again, the card provider knows when you travelled, where you went, how long it took (except on buses, where you only use the card when you board and not when you leave), and where, how, and how frequently you topped up the card. All of this appears to be harmless because we benefit from much of the technology and services, but to return to one of the original points of this section, if the security services wanted to build a profile of you, it would be extremely easy to combine credit/debit card, store card, travel card, email messages, and internet searches with closed-circuit television (CCTV) images.

A data aggregator could create a detailed portrait of our daily lives. They'd know where we live, where we work, and possibly what kind of work we do; who our partners and friends are; when and where we shop; what and where we eat and drink; where we go on vacation; what music and films we enjoy; what newspapers and magazines we read; what television shows we watch; what kind of car we drive and where we go in it; and what hobbies we have. To put it another way, there's very little about our personal lives that is truly private any longer.

The sophistication of home entertainment systems has increased. Televisions can link to the internet not only to allow for the download of viewing material, but also to give manufacturers with data about viewing patterns. In theory, this type of remote monitoring should only be done with the viewer's explicit consent, but there have been instances where manufacturers have submitted watching data without the viewer's knowledge.

From a personal standpoint, we should always be concerned that our personal information is properly maintained and used. When our credit card company calls to question a transaction that appears to be outside of our normal spending pattern, we are grateful that they took the time to do so in order to keep us safe. As a result, we should be more cautious about the information we give out to others – information that could be abused or misused for their benefit at our expense; and reactively, if we suspect abuse or misuse of our information or credentials, we should change passwords and notify financial institutions right away. There are several reasons why we should be aware of cyber occurrences, plan to defend ourselves and our organisations from cyber-attacks and be ready to respond if they occur from a commercial standpoint. Managing risk, including the hazards of cyber-attacks, whether accidental or malicious, and whether as individuals or enterprises, is nothing short of best practise. Corporates (and board members) do have fiduciary responsibilities in this regard.

Customers have a right to expect businesses to protect their personal information when they give it to them for whatever reason, and they must have confidence that it will not be misused – in other words, strict respect to data protection laws. In highly regulated industries, businesses may be required to demonstrate compliance with national or EU law, international standards such as ISO/IEC 27001, and industry standards such as the Payment Card Industry Data Security Standard (PCIDSS), the US Health Insurance Portability and Accountability Act (HIPAA), and the Sarbanes– Oxley Act. As a means of gaining a competitive edge, businesses should be able to demonstrate excellent security practises. Some larger organisations may use ISO/IEC 27001 certification to demonstrate this, whilst smaller organisations that employ small-to-medium enterprises (SMEs) may use the UK government's Cyber Essentials and/or Cyber Essentials Plus programmes.

Rather than keeping our memories on paper, we now store them digitally. Letters, postcards, and photographs are all files on our computer, and when we compare information about us to footprints in the sand or an aircraft's vapour trail, the digital footprint pales in comparison. While physical footprints are washed away by the tide and vapour trails vanish, we continuously generate remnants that may last an eternity.

What Is Stopping Us?

Life is not as straightforward as we would like it to be, and there are a variety of impediments or barriers to meeting our privacy and security expectations, particularly for individuals, small businesses, and SMEs. Cyber security is sometimes regarded as a highly specialised subject, and many individuals and small businesses believe they lack the essential knowledge or skills to comprehend or carry out the work required to protect themselves against cyber-attack. Organizations of all sizes usually lack the personnel resources to devote to this type of job. The senior management team of the organisation may not fully comprehend the need of excellent cyber security and how it may benefit their business, as well as the fact that the data and hence the information held by the organisation belongs to them, not the IT department. When we look at the cyber security standards that have been developed, it appears that many of them are tailored toward larger organisations and multinationals. The Cyber Essentials scheme, on the other hand, addresses this for smaller businesses. Many SMEs outsource their IT, and many of the outsourced companies are likewise small businesses with limited cyber security expertise. When a company is able to devote resources to internal IT projects, it is common to anticipate that those employees will also be responsible for cyber security. This is a significant blunder since it may go against one of the most important concepts of cyber security: the separation of roles. Because it controls the data, information, and strategic direction, the organisation must determine the cyber security requirement. To translate the demand into technical policies, the IT department must follow best security practises. The human resources (HR) function must then provide employee training and education to fulfil the demand in collaboration with the IT and business functions. When the IT function is outsourced, there is a propensity to neglect or minimise the importance of effective cyber security in the outsourced contract, because people negotiating the contract may not have a thorough understanding of the requirement, or they may remove it because it is an unnecessary cost. When a security function is outsourced, it is frequently a kind of duty abdication rather than delegation. The guiding principle is that while organisations can outsource information security implementation and management, they cannot export ownership responsibility. The cost of establishing and implementing a cyber security framework that is enough to defend the organisation will be higher and securing capital or operating budget approval may be difficult. The capacity to design a strong cyber security strategy is somewhat dependent on the organization's grasp of information security risk management, which is not always the case. Organizations can also evaluate their cyber security capabilities using one of the Capability Maturity Models, which are commonly used in software development but have many similarities in the cyber security world.

In the information and cyber security areas, there are literally dozens (if not hundreds) of standards. Some are broad in scope and apply to a variety of security issues, while others are narrowly focused and only pertain to a single technology. There's also the risk that, especially for larger organisations, obtaining ISO/IEC 27001 certification means they're entirely secure and all they have to do now is 'keep turning the handle.' This is far from the truth, as complacency is frequently the cause of both organisations and individuals failing to notice a new threat or weakness and being successfully targeted as a result. Although there are several outstanding standards in the cyber security industry (most notably the US National Institute of Standards and Technology (NIST), BSI, and ISO/IEC standards), few of them are easily adaptable to SMEs. This is where the government of the United Kingdom's Cyber Essentials scheme shines. Implementation guidelines are also more suited to larger organisations, making it difficult for SMEs to adapt them to their specific circumstances. Many worldwide standards imply that organisations would have established some higher-level processes and procedures that many smaller organisations would not be able to do. Small businesses may not be able to commit to the degree of investment required to attain ISO/IEC 27001 certification.

SECTION 2:

CYBER VULNERABILITIES

Cyber Fundamentals

A vulnerability is simply a flaw that can be used to launch an attack on a network, system, or service. While we may not be able to prevent risks and hazards from occurring, we can often take efforts to decrease or even eliminate vulnerabilities. Some vulnerabilities are inherent in the asset, such as the capacity to overwrite or delete data on magnetic media, while others are the result of an unintentional or deliberate action or inaction, such as the inability to perform regular backups. Vulnerabilities, as well as the controls we might apply to address them, exist in a variety of shapes and sizes. The majority of them are caused by a lack of policies, processes, and procedures, or a failure to follow them. Technical flaws are far less common, but they can be quite dangerous. People-related vulnerabilities, as well as environmental vulnerabilities, are key concerns.

Vulnerabilities in policies, processes, and procedures are all too frequent. Despite the fact that many organisations have robust rules and procedures in place – either to ensure that the right things happen or to ensure that the wrong things don't happen – they are frequently ignored or given lip regard.

The lack of a company to have a comprehensive information security policy ranks first on the list of vulnerabilities. Security rules do not need to be long or complicated; they should simply explain what formalities the organisation requires and make it apparent that everyone must follow them.

The second key area of weakness is the lack of, or badly drafted, access control policies, and the lack of a sufficient policy, or one that is not well conveyed to workers, may have serious consequences. Access to systems, apps, and information should only be granted if the user has a legitimate business need for them, and it should always be approved by their line manager.

Another vulnerability linked to this is a lack of access control for users who change roles or leave the company. When someone changes roles, their access to systems, applications, and information is usually ignored. Role-based authentication is one way to tackle this, in which a user is granted access based on both their job function and their identification, rather than just their identity. When a user leaves an organisation, their access rights should be immediately revoked so that they cannot access the network or systems.

Poor password management is another area of weakness, including the failure to enforce regular password changes along with a test of password strength. However, the National Institute of Standards and Technology (NIST) recently determined that frequent changes are inconvenient for users and that strength checkers may not be adequately robust. Instead, new recommendations are being developed1 that rank password length and hashing method2 as more user-friendly by putting the responsibility of verification on the verifier rather than the user.

The ongoing use of default factory-set accounts and passwords for new and upgraded computers is a typical issue. Many people in the hacking community are aware of them, and they spread among the community. Failure to change or hide wireless network identities or service set identifiers (SSIDs) allows an attacker to pinpoint target networks, and if default administrator passwords have not been changed, or the security level has not been enhanced, these provide a highly appealing entry point into an organization's network.

Then there's the trend of embedding user IDs and passwords within applications to allow one system to connect to another. This is a highly problematic technique, because a change on one system might quickly cause application failures on another.

Many organisations fail to protect mobile devices, whether these are supplied by the organisation, or brought in by the users themselves (bring your own device; BYOD) (bring your own device; BYOD). Mobile devices, unless properly configured, are unsecure and easily lost, misplaced, or stolen, putting both the device and the network to which it can connect at risk.

In bigger organisations, network segregation is frequent, with different networks built according to business requirements, including confidentiality, integrity, and availability. An organisation with a substantial research capability, for example, might put this on a different network than that used for finance or general administration. Failure to restrict network access based on use is a common vulnerability that can allow users to access resources to which they do not have access.

A common weakness is the lack of a clear workstation and explicit screen rules. Employees who leave private materials in plain view, or who fail to log out of or protect their workstation when they are away from their desk, may face disciplinary action.

Unauthorized access to administrator accounts is a common flaw. Administration rights should be restricted to only trained and authorised employees, and this should apply to both user PCs and central systems. Administrators should also have two identities, one with administrator rights for such tasks and a second 'standard' user account for everyday tasks including email, internet access, and office work.

It is standard procedure for businesses to test new or updated software, including patches, before releasing them into a production or general use environment. Untested software can cause not just operational concerns if it fails to perform as expected, but it can also have a knock-on impact when used in conjunction with other programmes, culminating in an embarrassing chain of events.

Failure to restrict the use of system utilities like a terminal console application – typically by setting access privileges within the user's profile – can lead to users performing actions that are harmful to their own device as well as other systems, applications, or information within the organisation.

In some cases, employees may allow attackers to take advantage of information that they would not ordinarily have access to. This relates to access control, where role-based access to information may be advantageous. Staff should not be put in a position where they can not only issue requisitions for items, but also authorise them to be purchased.

Inadequate network management, which includes monitoring of hacking and intrusion attacks, will result in successful attacks and intrusions being overlooked, with little or no information available until much later.

Unprotected public network connections, which offer an attacker simple access to an organization's network, are the source of many attacks, including the usage of shared computers in public venues such as internet cafés and the use of unapproved and potentially unsecured wireless access points (WAPs).

Users of an organization's networks will occasionally find ways to circumvent the organization's security protocols by connecting their devices to sections of the network to which they do not have access. This can be accomplished by connecting to a 'rogue' wireless access point to which they have unlimited access. One of the primary concerns with this is that the security settings of such wireless access points may not be as rigorous as those of the organisation, and while users may be able to access the network, an attacker may be able to as well.

Malware protection software, particularly out-of-date antivirus software, makes an attacker's task considerably easier. Attackers will use whatever means of access at their disposal, and they are often aware of vulnerabilities in programmes and operating systems long before a fix is available. Delays in updating these programmes put a company vulnerable to cyber-attacks.

Failure to deploy software patches from manufacturers exposes operating systems and application software to attack.

Most businesses now back up their users' data on a regular basis. They are significantly less likely to verify that these backups are truly suitable for purpose and that data can be reliably restored from the backup medium. This is yet another significant flaw, because backup material that fails to meet its goal is just as bad as having no backup regime at all.

When storage media reaches the end of its useful life, it must be properly disposed of or wiped before being reused. There have been numerous reports in the press of customers who have purchased used computers only to discover that the hard drives still contain sensitive or confidential data that was not securely erased prior to the sale. Some organisations refuse to allow the resale of any magnetic media and insist on irreversible disposal.

The idea of allowing employees to bring their own device to work has gained traction since it can lower an organization's IT hardware costs. However, the lack of rigorous 'bring your own device' (BYOD) policies for its use, as well as their enforcement, can result in major security breaches, particularly when additional members of a user's family have access to the same device.

Inadequate change control can result in the distribution of software and updates to users, the creation of new systems and services, and the removal of redundant systems without complete analysis (and risk assessment) of the repercussions. Change control can easily be vested in one or two persons on a part-time basis in smaller networks, but as an organization's network grows, a full-time team with representatives from several business units may be required.

Online transactions and email correspondence must be subject to extensive tracking and non-repudiation in particular industries. This audit trail is incorporated into the running software in many programmes, and in the case of a dispute over "who did what" or "who said what," organisations that can show proof in their favour will significantly reduce their risk profile.

Users may mistakenly connect to a test system, resulting in failed transactions, if organisations that use large-scale systems and application testing prior to rollout fail to separate test and operational facilities.

It is not only good practise for organisations to include acceptable use statements in employment contracts, but it should be required, whether for permanent employees or external contractors, so that employees and contractors have no excuse for not knowing that they are not permitted to visit inappropriate websites, send or receive inappropriate emails, or post inappropriate material on social media or web blogs.

Operational management should minimise the uncontrolled copying of business information by users who don't require it — this is primarily an access control issue, although detecting such activity may fall under a separate management area. USB memory sticks and shared network drives are examples of this.

Technical Vulnerabilities

Technical vulnerabilities may be more difficult to detect, but they are frequently extremely damaging. These could also be termed policy, process, or procedure failures.

One of the most important challenges that exists today is poor coding procedures. Baby monitors, CCTV systems, home entertainment systems, and environmental management systems are among the internet-connected goods that have emerged as a result of the Internet of Things. Many of them have been found to have insufficient or no security in the application software that runs on the IoT device itself, as well as in any application that is used to operate it. Such flaws will almost certainly have disastrous effects, as an attacker can not only assault and take control of the device, but also utilise it as a steppingstone to other network devices. Even if a vulnerability is discovered and hopefully addressed, the chances of the rectified code being rolled out to the complete user population are slim, especially if a device has already been hacked. Poor coding practises are not confined to the IoT environment; they also influence operating systems and applications, especially when combined with back doors that make it easier for a coder to test code.

Poor coding practise sometimes stems from a lack of clarity in the product or service's needs. Although it has long been believed that it is always better to build security into a product from the start rather than trying to patch it in afterwards, many organisations continue to do so.

Poor quality assurance and testing is easy to envisage, such as when a programmer writing software for an IoT device is also responsible for its functionality testing, exacerbating the problem (given the lack of a security requirement in the product's specification).

Physical And Environmental Vulnerabilities

Physical and environmental vulnerabilities will have an impact in some locations, and the consequences can be devastating. Physical access to critical buildings and sensitive locations within them should be properly managed, but this is all too often not the case, leaving the door open for an attacker to enter unnoticed. Theft is a common motivation for this type of entry, which can be facilitated by skilled social engineering and the distraction of security personnel, but it can also allow an attacker to implant malware into a system.

In addition to gaining entry to the equipment room, a breach in security can allow an intruder to obtain access to specific systems, allowing malware to be injected. When a number of systems are housed in a same rack space, gaining physical access to one instantly grants an attacker physical access to all of the others. Although locking equipment cabinets is a simple solution, keys are commonly forgotten in the cabinet lock.

Single points of failure (SPoFs) are a key vulnerability for any organisation that provides services over the internet, or even internally to its employees. The main computer system, its operating system, software applications, firewall technologies, network connectivity, web servers, and any front-end load balancing solutions are all included in these SPoFs. The service design must account for the likelihood of any of these components failing, resulting in a service failure as a whole, and the design must be prepared to avoid this.

Key systems are almost always housed in controlled environments, such as computer and equipment rooms with heating, ventilation, and air conditioning (HVAC), but this creates a potential single point of failure because everything depends on the environmental controls to keep the temperature and humidity constant.

The risk is minor if these are kept within stated ranges, but if the temperature changes, especially if it rises over suggested levels, equipment may stop working. Some data centres, on the other hand, now run their equipment rooms at somewhat higher temperatures than are acceptable for people, recognising that a few degrees higher in temperature will not cause difficulties but will save a significant amount of money in the long run.

Because power is so important, it is the main weakness of all systems. While a loss of power for any length of time can cause serious difficulties, equipment is far more prone to being turned on and off repeatedly, and it is much more likely to fail catastrophically.

Nowadays, no self-respecting company with a significant IT infrastructure would consider anything other than an uninterruptible power supply system to power their critical computer room or data centre, which would be backed up by a standby generating system. Other critical services, such as those used by the supporting operations staff, are frequently powered by such systems.

People Vulnerabilities

We should level with ourselves. We are only human after all. People make errors. All businesses must now pay more attention to the human aspect of security, particularly internal vulnerabilities. Security breaches can result in damage to a company's reputation and brand image, as well as a loss of revenue and customer base, the leakage of intellectual property and commercial information to competitors, fines, and criminal prosecution.

Advances in information technology have increased the size of potential breaches and the speed with which their consequences spread. At the same time, cybercriminals have become more organised and sophisticated, aided by a black market in stolen data and malware toolkits. Every business must be aware of the threats it faces, constantly assess and update its security procedures, and be watchful in the event of a breach.

In some ways, this isn't entirely new. Knights wore armour comprised of articulated metal plates, chain mail, and padding on the battlefield in the Middle Ages. Each plate had a specific function and was formed accordingly, but it also had to link with its neighbours in a flexible manner. The armour's components had to cover all of the knight's strategic bodily parts such as head, chest, arms, and so on, while yet allowing him to function as a fighting machine.

Any weakness would be immediately exploited by lower-level, less well-equipped, but more numerous and nimble adversaries. As a result, the armour's design had to strike a balance between increasing strength and coverage on the one hand, and minimising the impact on movement, vision, and communication on the other. Cost, as well as the display of wealth and power, played a significant role.

The modern organisation, like the knight of old, relies on the harmonious interaction of disparate elements, which are frequently classed under the headings of 'people,' 'processes,' and 'technology.' An adversary seeking to attack the organization's information security will use the simplest method possible, which frequently involves influencing people or exploiting their mistakes. It's tempting to infer that people are "awful for security," and that problems should be solved by automation or strict discipline. This, however, would be a mistake. Overall, employees do not deliberately breach security; rather, the ease with which attackers can exploit them is generally the result of poorly designed technology and processes, as well as a lack of sufficient training.

Because many security experts are technologists, it's natural for us to consider users as an unavoidable evil from whom technology must be protected. The other viewpoint that it is human to make mistakes, but it takes a machine to completely screw things up is also widely held, and equally incorrect. The underlying issue is that hardware and humans have very distinct qualities, not that one side is good and the other is wicked. People will make mistakes, interpret instructions differently depending on their mood, and use their common sense for good or bad, whereas machines will perform the same task faithfully day after day, regardless of whether the results make sense. It's no surprise, then, that many of the most serious security issues come at the point where humans and technology collide.

The process is the organization's third component. If an organisation is compared to a computer system, business processes are the programmes that dictate what it does. These programmes 'run' on two separate forms of hardware: people and IT, each with its own set of advantages and disadvantages. Parts of a business process can be automated for predictability and efficiency, but it must be stated prescriptively and in great detail. If the process designer overlooks security flaws, the predictability of the IT system becomes a weakness that an attacker can exploit - a weakness that can be exploited repeatedly in a short period of time.

People, on the other hand, have the ability to decipher instructions. This is both a strength and a flaw at the same time. A person can cope with instructions that are poorly phrased and adapt them to the conditions they are confronted with. There are a variety of people-related vulnerabilities, some of which are caused by the organization's lack of training and knowledge, while others are caused by people's incapacity to think and behave logically or follow instructions.

The best definition of social engineering is an act that persuades someone to do something that is not in their or their organization's best interests. Persuading someone to reveal personal or secret information is part of this.

People are commonly victims of social engineering or coercion, which occurs when an attacker, who may have conducted research on the target, is able to acquire their trust by flattering them or presenting an enticement that the individual is likely to accept.

Many cyber-attackers strive hard to improve their social engineering skills, as assistance from within an organisation can save them a lot of time and effort. The employment of so-called 'dark patterns,' in which the user is enticed to perform an action they did not plan, is one kind of social engineering.

One of the most serious flaws is a lack of awareness. Providing people with free malware-infected memory sticks is an incredibly successful method of spreading malware. This can be accomplished not just by handing them out at conferences and fairs, but also by putting them on the ground near the home or workplace of a target user. People would cheerfully plug these into their computers, thinking they're getting something for nothing, without thinking about the probable implications.

One of the most common forms of vulnerability is failure to follow corporate standards and best practises. Computer users, particularly those working in a corporate context, will find themselves confined by the organization's policies, processes, and procedures, and may attempt to undermine or work around them. This is sometimes due to their own laziness, as doing things correctly costs work; other times, they simply do not understand the need or disagree with the requirement.

People writing down essential passwords, especially passwords for root access to systems, and exchanging passwords with co-workers who have forgotten their own, or who should not have access in the first place, are common problems.

When using an application or service, users will occasionally use a simple password (for example, 1234). Although good password management systems should prevent this, users will occasionally find ways to get around them. Passwords that are easily guessed or broken, such as one's mother's maiden name, are another vulnerability in this area.

Another flaw is a lack of response to training and awareness. It's critical that this isn't a one-time event, but rather a continuous process, so that users are kept up to date on security issues they should be aware of and continue to be trained in proper procedures. Some areas of user behaviour, however, will continue to demand line management action if they do not comply, and some organisations penalise employees who neglect their training on a regular basis.

Employees can also (and do) detect concerns and questionable conduct, utilise common sense, and take initiative to intervene or ask for help. Unfortunately, if instructions do not appear to make sense on first reading or are inconvenient, people will adjust, if not entirely ignore, accurately and precisely expressed instructions. However, from the attacker's perspective, the most important aspect of them is that they may be modified.

It is critical to address human weaknesses. This refers to security flaws in an organisation caused by human qualities and behaviours. Due to the interdependence of the three organisational factors, we must also evaluate the impact of procedures and technology on people's contributions to security. To begin, we must provide opportunities for people to contribute positively to security through awareness campaigns, education, encouragement, and empowerment. Second, we must create systems, incentives, and security policies that minimise conflicts of interest and make it simple for individuals to act safely. Finally, we must create technical solutions that have simple user interfaces and offer people with intuitive models of their functionality.

Human error is still the biggest security flaw. Technical security controls make it significantly easier to secure technology. Human mistake is a problem that businesses will continue to face.

Let's start with carelessness as an example of how human nature can lead to security vulnerabilities. There isn't a week that goes by without news of a laptop or USB stick carrying critical information being left on a train or being taken from the back seat of a car. Electronic technology today is extremely portable and capable of storing massive amounts of data. Employees are explicitly encouraged to take use of this portability, to work on the go and from home, thus they are unlikely to be chastised if they do so. We're not just referring to laptops here. It's easy to underestimate the amount of data kept on smart phones and other gadgets that we use in both our professional and personal lives.

People used to just fill their briefcase with the papers they required for the day when they went to a meeting. Everything else was abandoned. We can now bring everything except the kitchen sink with us, including all of our correspondence on every issue, every report that's come across our desk, and much more.

It's a benefit in certain ways. There's no way you're going to a meeting only to realise you've forgotten the most important document. In other aspects, however, it is a major issue. You're putting a lot more at danger by taking so much with you. The most obvious solution is to only bring what you require. It's tempting to carry more information just in case, or since downloading entire databases is easier than extracting individual elements. Keeping a backup copy on a USB stick may seem like a good idea, but it also doubles the odds that the data will be lost. This is also true for paper copies, and while a paper document has less information than a computer, the information is visible to everybody.

Remote access capabilities have vastly improved and become far more user-friendly. Furthermore, public hotspots are becoming increasingly common, and some trains now have Wi-Fi. (However, keep in mind that 'free public Wi-Fi' isn't necessarily what it appears to be.)

This eliminates the need for people to carry around so much data. The concept is straightforward: data is significantly safer when it is stored on central servers that are adequately secured and controlled. As a result, the ideal choice is for people to leave it in place and access it remotely as needed.

But what about the data that people must bring with them? Full-disk encryption of built-in hard drives, as well as automatically enforced encryption of USB drives, are strongly recommended for this purpose. It may appear complex, but it is not difficult or expensive to accomplish. Hardware-based solutions that can protect whole discs to standards that considerably surpass most organisations' needs are available. Software-based data protection systems, which secure data file by file, are even less expensive. When compared to the falling prices of computer hardware, this may appear to be a lot. For example, a powerful laptop PC may be had for a few hundred pounds. But keep in mind that the data on a device can be significantly more valuable than the device itself. Encryption is a bargain in that setting.

Remember that the information is useful to both you and the thief. It might truly ruin your day if your only copy of the report you've been working on is on the laptop that has just gone missing! So, make a daily backup of your key work and keep the copy secure and separate from the original.

Finally, being cautious pays off. Leave valuable documents and equipment unattended and in plain sight. If you're travelling by car, secure your laptop in the boot rather than keeping it in plain sight in the passenger seat. Remember that corporate espionage is rampant – and sometimes state-sponsored – in certain foreign nations, so locked hotel rooms aren't safe. Also, when you're working, keep an eye on who's around you. Is it possible for the guy or woman in the seat behind you to see the important information on your screen? Also, be cautious about what you say on the phone in public. Consider the ramifications if a representative from one of your most vehement competitors sat at the adjacent table.

Staff can assist in reducing risk. To begin, do not carry any more data than is absolutely necessary. Encrypt discs and other data storage devices, second. Back up important files on a regular basis. Do not leave documents or equipment unattended. Always keep an eye out for prying eyes.

This takes us nicely to the subject of information disclosure by mistake. All we can do now is improve our preparation in order to avoid an accident. Even the heads of security-conscious organisations inadvertently reveal material that they were seeking to keep private. Every day, millions of people can be found on trains, in airport lounges, and in other public areas having private conversations and viewing private papers. It's all too easy to unknowingly be drawn into discussing private topics with strangers or co-workers in a social setting only to make oneself or one's job look fascinating.

It's frightening to learn how people read private documents on the train in front of the entire world. By not reading secret information in public areas, employees can reduce their risk. Second, avoid discussing private topics in public locations. Put secret documents in an envelope or, better yet, a secured case if you need to leave the office.

It is not intelligence to never make a mistake, but rather to react fast to correct errors. Computers will reliably follow instructions as long as they are clear and consistent. Humans may not perform what they are instructed if they do not see the benefit, but they will attempt to decipher ambiguous instructions and can deal in situations when instructions are not applicable.

Employees are frequently forced to choose between getting on with their jobs and causing delays and discomfort by adhering to security policy. In a workplace where many employees share the same terminals, such as a business or a hospital, a policy that compels employees to utilise only their own individual accounts is an example of this. The temptation is to allow a colleague to perform a transaction during your session rather than logging off and on again if you're pressed for time or want to be helpful. Simply enforcing a policy, whether by technical methods or the prospect of punishment, might backfire. When employees are treated like a gear in the machine or a misbehaving child, they can feel demotivated and resentful. They may also associate the control measure with the policy, believing that if they figure out a means to get around the control, they aren't violating the policy. Furthermore, if a regulation is viewed as unneeded, petty, bureaucratic, or just incorrect, the entire topic of security is tarnished.

Naive productivity incentives can exacerbate the situation. Staff will devise clever ways to get around security measures that slow them down if rewards are based on the number of jobs processed. Worse, security will be viewed as a threat to genuine work rather than a significant contributor to the company's health.

Software, as well as other difficult-to-use and comprehend technology, can generate comparable issues. Staff must have a mental model of how the technology works in order to use their common sense and judgement in balancing security and productivity, for example. This is not at a profound technical level, but at a level that allows them to comprehend the implications of their actions and decisions.

It's all too simple for consumers to overlook a step or two if security equipment comes with a set of operating instructions that simply have to be followed without justification or explanation. If everything appears to be working and nothing unpleasant occurs, they will come to the logical conclusion that 'obviously those measures don't really matter.' But what if the missing steps were related to encrypting sensitive data on CDs that were going to be transmitted over the mail? Missing them won't matter if the envelope is delivered correctly 99 times out of 100, but the 100th time might result in significant fines and lost sales for the company, as well as possible dismissal for the employee.

The same may be said for business operations and security. Processes that are difficult for people to comprehend or utilise will lead to errors and well-intentioned improvements, as well as security flaws. Staff will be able to use their common sense and ingenuity productively when they encounter unique instances not covered in the instructions if the processes are well-designed and well-explained. You never know, they might even make some actual advancements.

There are no easy fixes or universal solutions here – managing, motivating, and educating people is a difficult task. The fundamental message is to do all possible to 'close the loop,' and to strive for continuous progress. Engage your employees, find out what they think, and, if possible, incorporate their suggestions. Observe actual behaviours and, where they differ from desired behaviours, try to understand why and respond to the issues at hand. We'll come back to these topics later.

Security measures operate best when they are incorporated into, rather than added to, the programmes and processes that people use. We should make certain that everyone understands why you're asking them to accomplish certain tasks. Make sure your procedures are in line with how people actually work. Finally, get feedback and act on it.

Password policies are a fascinating case study in security procedure design. Biometrics, smart cards, and other technologies are being used by Microsoft and other providers in place of passwords. Many organisations' systems, however, will continue to rely on users and passwords to restrict who has access to their networks and IT systems.

A password must be remembered by its owner, yet to all intents and purposes be a random jumble of characters to anybody else in order to be effective in terms of security. Unfortunately, people frequently use passwords that are simple to remember — and almost as simple to guess.

By using passwords like '1a2b3c,' 'iloveyou,' 'qwerty,' and even 'password,' many people leave the digital equivalent of a key under the doormat. '123456' is usually the most common. Given the size of most people's digital footprints these days, it's likely that many less popular passwords would have been easy to figure out for hackers and fraudsters. People frequently use phrases linked with their lives as passwords, such as their birthplace or the names of their children or pets, expecting that strangers would not be aware of these details. The problem is that such information is rapidly being shared on social media sites and in other public places. People also have a habit of using the same password for everything, so a breach of security on a fun website could lead to a criminal gaining access to your bank accounts or work e-mail.

Organizations that take security seriously restrict people's options. They demand that passwords contain letters and numbers, uppercase and lowercase characters, special characters such as percent, and *, and that they be longer than a certain length. Furthermore, they demand that passwords be changed on a regular basis.

While this makes it harder for others to guess the password, it also makes it extremely difficult to remember. You must not, of course, write it down.

A password's strength is determined by several factors, including length, complexity, and randomness. It will utilise the keyboard to the fullest extent feasible, including not only upper- and lower-case letters and numbers, but also punctuation marks and symbols when permitted. It will also be as long as feasible — eight characters is commonly considered the bare minimum. However, password strength and security are not synonymous. Strength makes the password tough to guess, but if it forces you to write down the passwords, for example, it may actually increase the likelihood of leak.

Whether writing down a password list is an issue or not depends on where the list is kept. People who are serious about keeping a list use a little piece of paper and keep it in their wallet or pocketbook, where they would keep other valuable items. They'll be notified as soon as they're lost or stolen, and they'll be able to take appropriate action.

A safer approach is to keep log-in data for individual apps and websites in a Password Management Utility or an encrypted document on your PC, making sure the password that opens your electronic safe is strong. An alternative method is to establish a system for creating passwords that is difficult to crack rather than trying to remember individual passwords.

A good strategy is to choose phrases that you'll remember, such as the first lines of favourite songs. Use easy-to-remember rules to replace some of the lowercase letters with capital letters, numbers, or symbols. Add characters or numbers to each site or application's password to make it unique. Choose a system that derives the characters from the name of the website or software you want to access. You might select the name's first two characters, then the number of characters it includes. Make a list of clues to help you remember the phrases and techniques you choose. Keep the piece of paper in a secure location, such as your wallet or purse. Change your passwords on a regular basis - every 90 days, for example. Remember, you don't have to make drastic changes. You may simply change the phrase that serves as the 'root' of your passwords while maintaining the same rules for substituting characters and linking passwords to websites.

A variety of password management applications are also available for technical support. These can be used to create strong passwords and securely store them. Then all you have to remember is the single password that grants you access to the password management software.

It is normal for employees to trust people they meet at work – especially those who are, or appear to be, colleagues, clients, or suppliers – and to try to aid them if they require assistance. We learn at our mother's knee that it is courteous to hold the door open for the person coming behind us. Even if we can't see their pass, it's most likely hidden beneath their jacket or in a pocket.

However, that well-dressed businessman hurrying through the security door could very well be planning industrial espionage. It's also crucial for folks to know that theft isn't the only issue you're dealing with when it comes to security. By bringing equipment into your business, fraudsters can steal money from your company. They might be allowed into the building if they dress as cleaning employees. They might connect hardware bugs to computer keyboard sockets once inside, then leave with nothing. The devices would send keystrokes to fraudsters over time. Criminals would gradually learn everything they needed to move large sums of money into their accounts, including login codes, passwords, and client account information. Fortunately, the authorities were made aware of the situation, and any attempted wire transfers were prevented.

Even IT helpdesk security professionals find it difficult to ignore the cries of damsels (and their male counterparts) in distress. When someone phone to say they'll be gone for a few days and need to prepare things for an important meeting but can't remember their password, new ones are issued so they can get what they need.

This is an example of social engineering, a well-known technique for persuading people to provide sensitive information.

Phishing is the term for an old-fashioned con trick that is carried out over e-mail. Every month, tens of billions of spoof e-mails are sent. Each pretends to be from a genuine organisation – such as a bank – and includes a very similar request: the receiver must visit a website to verify his or her username, password, and other information.

Most people are now aware of the problem, which is fortunate because the flood of e-mails shows no signs of abating. Every year, however, a small percentage of people make the mistake of doing as they are told. They go to the fraudster's website, provide the information, and then pay the price. Every year, cybercriminals make billions by duping victims.

This type of attack's new variations can be exceedingly complex and difficult to detect. Spear phishing as opposed to the usual e-mail scam, is more targeted and may, for example, be directed at the employees of a certain organisation. By include company lingo and the names of executives and department heads in the e-mail, it can be quite convincing. Even more targeted is 'whale phishing,' which targets specific 'big fish,' such as CEOs (yes, I know whales are mammals, but that's what it's called). Spoof subpoenas and tax notifications are examples fake whaling assaults. The executive, panicked or enraged at the prospect of legal action, clicks on an embedded link to a realistic-looking website. Those who have been targeted may never realise that key-logging software has been installed on their computers, capturing everything they type, including passwords, and granting access to sensitive commercial information.

It's not just e-mail that you need to keep an eye on. Other channels, such as instant messaging and social media, can be used to carry out the same basic attacks.

It's also incredible what people would do for a freebie. An annual experiment was done outside Liverpool Street station in central London for several years. If office staff completed a survey, they were given a chocolate bar. They were asked for numerous forms of personal information, including passwords, in the survey, and a large percentage of them responded positively. Because no one checked the passwords, it's possible that some of the subjects deceived the experimenters by providing phoney ones. Even Nevertheless, it appears that a little reward, when presented in the correct context, can blind people to huge risks.

Another experiment involves dispersing USB memory sticks over a company's campus, as though they had been dropped by accident. When they were inserted into a PC, they included a harmless software payload that simply transmitted a message back to the experimenters. They may, however, have been carrying malware that could have brought down the company network, stolen information, or provided back door access that could be abused later. People threw caution to the wind once more when they saw something for free.

We should all participate in frequent cyber awareness training to help protect our employees. Make no assumptions – double-check that people are exactly who they appear to be or claim to be. Be on the lookout for social engineering, spam, and phishing scams. If you're not sure where something came from, don't plug it into a computer.

The importance of awareness and training cannot be overstated. People can only assist in the prevention of security breaches if they are aware of the risks and are taught secure behaviours as part of their regular work training. An organisation must foster a culture in which employees share responsibility for defending the firm against attack — one in which everyone understands how to act responsibly, is aware of possible risks, and knows what to do in the event of a security breach.

It is critical that security training not only teaches what to do, but also why. Effective security, of course, is a business enabler and enhances the corporate brand — it inspires customer trust and has been known to assist in the closing of many key deals. The difficulty is that this is frequently not communicated, resulting in employees only knowing the 'what' and not the 'why.'

Security breaches may have a huge impact on an organization's brand and bottom line, so it's also crucial for people to realise that.

Senior teams must be aware of their personal accountability under international law, as well as the necessity to comply with legislation such as the US Sarbanes Oxley (SOX) Act, which was enacted in the wake of financial scandals like Enron, WorldCom, and Arthur Andersen. Top executives may perceive security as an unnecessary expense and must be persuaded that it can improve Return on Investment (ROI) and boost the company's bottom line. Middle managers, particularly those in sales and marketing, must understand that a strong security strategy can assist complete deals as a result of increased client trust. The broader staff should be made aware of the dangers and encouraged to 'keep the door locked,' both literally and digitally. This covers everything from safeguarding their laptops and BlackBerrys to ensuring that passwords are changed on a regular basis and that the last person to leave a building sets the alarm. Computer-based training is a low-cost solution to keep people's knowledge and skills current.

Beyond that, it's critical that everyone, starting at the top, is seen as being invested in the organization's security. If executives, senior and middle management, do not completely support an awareness and training effort, it will fail. This requires more than just beautiful words and speeches; leaders must be seen to model the safe behaviours they preach to others.

IT literacy at the board level, insistence on effective backup and access control mechanisms, readiness to spend money, and regular involvement on security issues are examples of positive behaviours indicating a high priority. Wanting protection without being willing to pay for it, failing to act after a security breach, having a poor knowledge of technological difficulties, and paying insufficient attention to developing employee awareness are all examples of low-priority behaviours.

It's crucial for managers to respond appropriately to security breaches. The vast majority of e-crime is caused or enabled by people who did not intend to harm others but did so by accident.

The lesson here is straightforward: if you want to keep people on your side, you must not 'criminalise' anyone who makes a simple mistake. There's a risk that issues will be swept under the rug and allowed to fester until they become very serious. Rather, an open and supportive environment is required to encourage people to 'fess up.' That way, the organisation will be able to learn from its mistakes and close stable doors before valuable horses bolt or are stolen. People's willingness to report problems is determined by their faith in the reporting system, which could be run by their employer, an independent agency, or a government agency. They will be concerned not only about being punished and prosecuted, but also about protecting their identities if they report the failings and transgressions of others. The aviation industry has had great success with reporting schemes that encourage employees to report safety-related incidents.

Security teams must make certain that everyone is trained in security. Explain both the "what" and the "why." Refresher courses should be held on a regular basis. The CEO sets the tone for security. He or she must set an example for others to follow. Allow people to easily report mistakes to avoid a blame culture.

An information security awareness programme will serve as a focal point and driving force for a variety of information security awareness, training, and instructional activities, some of which may already be in place but might be better coordinated and more successful. Important recommended recommendations, or practises, for securing information resources will be communicated through the awareness programme. It will provide anyone who need to know with broad and specialised information about information security risks and controls. Individuals will be made aware of their obligations in terms of information security. Individuals must be encouraged to follow recommended rules or procedures by security personnel. A robust security culture will emerge from a good awareness programme, with a broad understanding and dedication to information security. It will make existing information security measures more consistent and effective, as well as encourage the implementation of cost-efficient solutions. The major financial benefits of an effective programme are reduced costs directly (e.g., data damaged by viruses) and indirectly (e.g. reduced need to investigate and fix breaches); these are the key financial benefits of an effective programme. Awareness programmes and mandatory training are crucial, but they can only go so far. Training is most effective when it is reinforced by experience on a regular basis, which is a difficulty in the case of security. The absence of negative events, rather than the occurrence of positive ones, is what defines successful security. As a result, there are few opportunities to reinforce positive behaviour. As previously stated, except in cases of deliberate intent or blatant recklessness, punishing employees involved in security breaches is not a good idea. On an individual and organisational level, it encourages secrecy and obstructs learning.

Measuring the effectiveness of awareness and training campaigns can be difficult for similar reasons. However, it must be completed. It would be all too simple to spend money on posters, websites, and computer-based training and then sit back and relax, thinking "job done." It's far better to take a scientific approach to the problem. To begin, figure out what you're actually aiming to improve. Are you attempting to cut down on theft? Or is it a case of information leakage? Or is it a case of deception? Apart from anything else, this will help you focus your campaign. Then figure out how to put a number on the problem. Establish a starting point and monitor how it changes as the campaign develops. After then, keep measuring it because the benefits may wane as memories fade. You may avoid having a too narrow focus by adopting a variety of different success measures. You should examine your measures on a regular basis, as priorities and the nature of the dangers your company faces may vary.

If the data isn't too sensitive, publishing security metrics within your company can help engage employees. People are more motivated if they can see that their efforts are paying off. The ultimate goal should be to fully engage your employees in a programme of continuous improvement that improves enterprise information security performance. Here's an example of a hypothetical achievement level programme, given in the form of a capacity maturity model:

Ad hoc: There are no formal awareness or training programmes. Processes and procedures are, at best, sporadic.

Aware: A coordinated campaign to raise awareness of security risks, threats, and pitfalls among all employees. All employees have access to the security policies, which are documented.

Trained: Individual and team roles are trained in job-specific security procedures, which are defined, recorded, and taught as part of the training process.

Educated: Employees have a basic grasp of security threats and controls, as well as risk management strategies, which allows them to make sensible, well-informed judgments in their daily job and in unusual situations.

People across the organisation are empowered to make individual contributions to the continual enhancement of enterprise security, and they are trusted to do so. It is critical to assess the efficacy of public awareness and training programmes. To achieve continuous improvement, we must engage and involve our employees. The best method to dealing with the problem is to design-out the possibility of human error resulting to cybersecurity breaches. Human error will not occur if the chance for it does not there (think of automatic rather than user-installed security software upgrades).

Confidentiality, Integrity, and Availability (CIA) are the three types of operational risk that security is primarily concerned with.

Standards based on risk management principles, such as ISO27001, give best-practice guidance in creating, establishing, operating, and improving institutions and procedures. Information Security Management Systems are what they're called.

It is, nevertheless, as important to consider security when designing typical business procedures. Security is sometimes the 'Cinderella' need, added after the fact as an afterthought or as a result of a breach or near-miss. As a result, conflicts between security and other factors, such as productivity, go unnoticed and unaddressed.

Security procedures would be classified as 'supporting tasks' rather than 'production tasks' by human factors experts. Production tasks are concerned with the core day-to-day value production activity, and anything that interferes with them is promptly identified and remedied. Supporting chores are generally beneficial in the long run, although they can be regarded as 'getting in the way' in the near term. Security procedures that demand time away from regular employment, physical exertion, or mental attention will be disregarded as a result. To counteract this trend, security must be integrated into people's daily work and business operations rather than being a hindrance.

We must determine the production activity's performance requirements and ensure that the security task does not severely affect productivity. Reduce the security task's physical and mental stress by choosing an interaction mode that complements the production task's activity (e.g., voice-based mechanisms, telephone-based interactions, or a hands-free mechanism, for tasks where both hands are occupied). Design for speed in security mechanisms that are used frequently; design for memorability in security mechanisms that are used infrequently (step- by-step user guidance, recognition-based interfaces). Reduce the chances of making a mistake. Human factors research, particularly research on human error, provides a wealth of information on how to design systems that reduce the frequency and impact of errors. Systems must be designed in such a way that a single human error does not result in major security issues. Encourage safe behaviour (in addition to – or as part of – productivity goals).

A better balance between human limitations and the desire for increased security must be found. There is a need for more research into the relationship between usability, security, and convenience perceptions. Bugs and disputes are the two most common causes of software insecurity. The conflicts he's referring to are those between the desires for more bells and whistles, a faster time to market, lower costs, and increased security. I would add bad usability as a distinct concern to them.

You'll have an uphill battle no matter how much money you spend trying to educate people about information security if your systems and processes are difficult for them to understand or use. There are two approaches to the problem that should be treated as complementary approaches that should be used in tandem. One school of thought is that we should not allow users to do bad or stupid things: If a policy is mandatory, automate its enforcement if at all practicable. If a decision is too difficult for the ordinary user to make, it may be preferable to impose a safe (but sub-optimal) option. Consider developing user classes depending on degrees of competence, with expert users having more discretion.

The alternative is to assist the user in making good decisions: if user judgement or decision-making is required or desired, make it as simple as possible for the user to make the best choice. Provide a simple cause-and-effect model that the user can understand. Present all of the facts needed to make a decision in a clear and concise manner. Describe the consequences of each option. To reduce the chances of making a mistake, follow appropriate user-interface design concepts.

Human factors, human-computer interaction, man-machine interface design, usability, and other terms for the search for design principles guiding human interaction with technology are all maturing academic and applied fields of study. Some businesses even have their own usability testing labs. It's more of a black art than an engineering science in general, however there are some well-established concepts in particular fields. Car controls, aircraft cockpit design, and the now-familiar WIMP (window, icon, menu, pointing) interface on PCs are all examples. All of this is the product of years of co-evolution, in which designers responded to user feedback and users established mental models that allow them to utilise the controls intuitively.

Unfortunately, we still don't know exactly what it is about the way things are constructed that increases – or decreases – the likelihood that people would inadvertently perform things that expose organisations to attack.

Researchers from the University of Wisconsin-Madison and Copenhagen's IT University collaborated on a study that provided some insight on the situation. It discovered that security professionals are just as likely as average users to diverge from recommended practise when it comes to password selection. Experience, not expertise, was the most important factor. Advanced users were far more likely than beginners to choose 'strong' passwords, change them on a frequent basis, and so on, implying that exposure to the implications of security breaches enhances people's desire to get everything right.

The influence of security measures on users' capacity to complete tasks is something that demands special consideration. Firewalls are a good technique to control who and what can move between a company's private (and hopefully more secure) intranet and the public Internet. If the restrictions are too onerous, however, the likelihood that someone will simply copy files onto a memory stick and walk around what they perceive to be a roadblock increases. After all, people are often compensated based on their ability to do tasks, not on their adherence to security procedures.

'More research on how views of usability, security, and convenience are related is essential,' the researchers from the two universities concluded. Not the other way around, perceived usefulness, simplicity of use, and user happiness determine (proper) technology utilisation.'
'Adopting a participative approach to security analysis and design — including stakeholders in technical debates and decision-making surrounding security design' is one way. Stakeholders will gain a better understanding of security issues and will be able to communicate their own security requirements as a result of their participation.

In general, we can say that there are a few simple steps we can take to avoid issues. As part of day-to-day work, make security software simple to use. Better yet, include users in the design process. Allowing users to do bad or stupid things is not a good idea. Assist users in making good decisions.

Poor Governance Vulnerabilities

Despite the fact that many organisations have robust rules and procedures in place either to ensure that the right things happen or to ensure that the wrong things don't happen they are frequently ignored. This section outlines some of the most important policies and procedures that businesses should follow at a minimum.

The lack of a company to have a comprehensive information security policy ranks first on the list of vulnerabilities. Security rules do not need to be long or complicated; they should simply explain what formalities the organisation requires and make it apparent that everyone must follow them.

A formal access control policy, or one that is ineffective for the organization's purposes, is a primary source of issues. There will be serious consequences if there is no appropriate access control policy in place, or if one is not adequately conveyed to employees. Access to systems, apps, and information should only be granted when it is necessary for the user's job, and it should always be approved by their line manager.

Another vulnerability linked to this is a lack of access control for users who change roles or leave the company. When someone changes roles, their access to systems, applications, and information is usually ignored. Role-based authentication is one way to tackle this, in which a user is granted access based on both their job function and their identification, rather than just their identity. When a user leaves an organisation, their access rights should be immediately revoked so that they cannot access the network or systems.

Poor password management is one of the most common weaknesses. This has previously included failing to enforce regular password changes as well as a password strength test. However, the National Institute of Standards and Technology (NIST) determined that frequent changes are inconvenient for users and that strength checkers may not be adequately robust. Instead, new recommendations are being developed1 that rank password length and hashing method2 as more user-friendly by putting the responsibility of verification on the verifier rather than the user.

The ongoing usage of default factory-set accounts and passwords for new and upgraded computers is another incredibly widespread risk. Many people in the hacking community are aware of them, and they spread among the community. Failure to change or hide wireless network identities or service set identifiers (SSIDs) allows an attacker to pinpoint target networks, and if default administrator passwords have not been changed, or the security level has not been enhanced, these provide a highly appealing entry point into an organization's network.

Worse than continuing to utilise default settings is the inclination to allow one system to connect to another by embedding user IDs and passwords within programmes. This is a highly problematic technique, because a change on one system might quickly cause application failures on another.

Many businesses fail to safeguard mobile devices, whether they are provided by the company or brought in by employees (bring your own device; BYOD). Mobile devices, unless properly configured, are unsecure and easily lost, misplaced, or stolen, putting both the device and the network to which it can connect at risk. Mobile Device Management (MDM) is critical for ensuring that devices encrypt information and may be remotely deleted.

In bigger organisations, network segregation is frequent, with different networks built according to business requirements, including confidentiality, integrity, and availability. An organisation with a substantial research capability, for example, might put this on a different network than that used for finance or general administration. Failure to restrict network access based on use is a common vulnerability that can allow users to access resources to which they do not have access.

A common weakness is the lack of a clear workstation and explicit screen rules. Employees who leave private materials in plain view, or who fail to log out of or protect their workstation when they are away from their desk, may face disciplinary action.

Unauthorized access to administrator accounts is a common flaw. Administration rights should be restricted to only trained and authorised employees, and this should apply to both user PCs and central systems. Administrators should also have two identities, one with administrator rights for such tasks and a second 'standard' user account for everyday tasks including email, internet access, and office work.

It is standard procedure for businesses to test new or updated software, including patches, before releasing them into a production or general use environment. Untested software can cause not just operational concerns if it fails to perform as expected, but it can also have a knock-on impact when used in conjunction with other programmes, culminating in an embarrassing chain of events.

Failure to restrict the use of system utilities such as a terminal console application typically by setting access privileges within the user's profile can result in users carrying out activities that are harmful to their own device or to other systems, applications, or information within the organisation, despite being a relatively minor vulnerability.

All employees must keep their responsibilities separate. In some cases, employees may allow attackers to take advantage of information that they would not ordinarily have access to. This relates to access control, where role-based access to information may be advantageous. Staff should not be put in a position where they can not only issue requisitions for items, but also authorise them to be purchased.

Inadequate network management, particularly the monitoring of hacking and intrusion attacks, is another source of risk. This can lead to successful attacks and incursions being undetected, with little or no knowledge of their presence until much later.

Many assaults are also generated via unprotected public network connections, which offer an intruder simple access to an organization's network, such as the usage of shared computers in public places like internet cafes and the use of unapproved and perhaps insecure wireless access points (WAPs).

The uncontrolled use of user-owned wireless access points adds to the risk. Users of an organization's networks will occasionally find ways to circumvent the organization's security protocols by connecting their devices to sections of the network to which they do not have access. This can be accomplished by connecting to a 'rogue' wireless access point to which they have unlimited access. One of the primary concerns with this is that the security settings of such wireless access points may not be as rigorous as those of the organisation, and while users may be able to access the network, an attacker may be able to as well.

Malware security flaws and a failure to update safeguards might make a company vulnerable to attack. Malware protection software, particularly out-of-date antivirus software, makes an attacker's task considerably easier. Attackers will use whatever means of access at their disposal, and they are often aware of vulnerabilities in programmes and operating systems long before a fix is available. Delays in updating these programmes put a company vulnerable to cyber-attacks.

A lack of patching and updating might also leave an organisation vulnerable. Failure to install manufacturers' software patches, like failing to update malware protection software on a regular basis, leaves operating systems and application software vulnerable to attack.

Poor or untested backup and restore methods might expose a system to vulnerability. Most businesses now back up their users' data on a regular basis. They are significantly less likely to verify that these backups are truly suitable for purpose and that data can be reliably restored from the backup medium. This is yet another significant flaw, because backup material that fails to meet its goal is just as bad as having no backup regime at all.

Improper disposal of 'end of life' storage media can leave an organisation dangerously unprotected. When storage media reaches the end of its useful life, it must be properly disposed of or wiped before being reused. There have been numerous reports in the press of customers who have purchased used computers only to discover that the hard drives still contain sensitive or confidential data that was not securely erased prior to the sale. Some organisations refuse to allow the resale of any magnetic media and insist on irreversible disposal. There have been instances of computers being purchased with the previous user's data intact, as well as machines being left on trains without password security.

Inadequate "bring your own device" (BYOD) regulations can potentially expose a company to risk. The idea of allowing employees to bring their own device to work has gained traction since it can lower an organization's IT hardware costs. However, the lack of adequate policies for its use, as well as their enforcement, can result in major security breaches, particularly when other members of a user's family have access to the same device.

A virus that was carried in on a user's personal computer wreaked havoc on one of the author's acquaintances' organisations. The PC had been used by the user's daughter over the weekend, who had accidentally browsed a malware-infected website. The infection that resulted infected a huge portion of the company's network, and it took the IT department several days to clean up. The user, who had a prominent position within the company, was later warned, but the same thing happened the next week, and the user was barred from bringing in his own machine.

Inadequate change control and management procedures can result in software and patches being rolled out to users, new systems and services and network connections being established, and redundant systems being decommissioned without due thought (and risk assessment). Change control can easily be vested in one or two persons on a part-time basis in smaller networks, but as an organization's network grows, a full-time team with representatives from several business units may be required.

Audit trails that are insufficient can also generate problems. Online transactions and email correspondence must be subject to extensive tracking and non-repudiation in particular industries. This audit trail is incorporated into the running software in many programmes, and in the case of a dispute over "who did what" or "who said what," organisations that can show proof in their favour will significantly reduce their risk profile.

Separation of test and production is insufficient. Users may mistakenly connect to a test system, resulting in failed transactions, if organisations that use large-scale systems and application testing prior to rollout fail to separate test and operational facilities.

Companies can become increasingly vulnerable as a result of poor acceptable usage procedures. It is not only good practise for organisations to include acceptable use statements in employment contracts, but it should be required, whether for permanent employees or external contractors, so that employees and contractors have no excuse for not knowing that they are not permitted to visit inappropriate websites, send or receive inappropriate emails, or post inappropriate material on social media or web blogs.

Insider threats and unmanaged copying of corporate information can be caused by insufficient access controls and a lack of Data Loss Prevention (DLP). The uncontrolled copying of information by users who have no need for it should be limited by operational management - this is essentially an access control issue, but the detection of such activity may fall under a different management area. USB memory sticks and shared network drives are examples of this.

SECTION 3:

CYBER ATTACK VECTORS

Understand Your Attackers

The threat of a cyber-attack is multi-faceted, and we must attempt to comprehend and think like those who would seek to harm the organisation. Any individual or organisation that could gain from attacking an information asset must be considered as a potential threat source. Threat actors are frequently paid or pressured by threat sources to attack information assets on their behalf. Individuals or groups of individuals who carry out a cyber-attack are known as threat actors or agents. Actual attacks are described by threat actions. Surveillance, first activities, testing, and the final attacks are frequently not a single isolated event, but rather a series of distinct operations combining surveillance, initial activities, testing, and the final attacks. Danger analysis is the process of determining the severity of a threat, which can be investigated further in a formal risk management approach. Threat vectors, also known as attack vectors, are the tools, strategies, and mechanisms used by an attacker to attack a target. The effects or impacts of a cyber-attack are known as threat consequences or impacts.

While some assaults are more frequent than others, the severity of the consequences does not always reflect the type of organisation attacked or the chance of them occurring. Anyone or any organisation can be attacked, and most likely has been.

We need to identify the types of people and organisations who may launch cyber-attacks, as well as their likely reasons, before we can prepare to put preventative measures in place or develop the tools to respond to them. We will be much better equipped to cope with them if we have a thorough understanding of this area of cyber security.

In order to attain their goal, each assailant or criminal requires a purpose, means, and method. We must comprehend their motivation. There has to be a rationale for them to launch a cyber-attack, even if it appears to be in vain. The majority of cybercrime is motivated by profit, however there are some who attack networks for a variety of reasons, including retribution, establishing their perceived superiority, making a political statement, or simply being a nuisance. Then we need to figure out what they're up to. To mount a successful attack, an attacker must have a certain level of competence. Attackers with little or no talent will frequently fail in their attempts and will most likely be detected and prosecuted, whereas those with sufficient drive will persevere and improve their skills over time. Finally, we must take into account their techniques. Attackers with more experience will devise a strategy for their attack. This may necessitate an interim break-in, followed by extensive reconnaissance before the actual attack.

Some of these attackers will be lone wolves; others will be groups of lone wolves, often organised into a loose community; and yet others will be well-organized criminal gangs. Nation governments are on the other end of the scale, and while some will use the attack for pure espionage, others will have a far more sinister intent.

Script kiddies (skiddies), hacktivists, lone wolves, investigative journalists, small criminals, organised criminals, terrorists, insiders, or security agencies are all possible attackers. Another element to consider is the attacker's capabilities, which will differ greatly.

Let's start with attackers who come from outside our organisation and launch cyber-attacks. Skiddies are inexperienced skiers. They don't have to be young, but they should have some computing and cyber security experience and be willing to learn. This usually entails downloading free malware from the internet and attacking 'soft' targets with a lower risk of causing damage or being detected. Skiddies are often looked down upon by experienced hackers, despite the fact that this is where many of them began. On the other hand, hacktivists already have a cause to support. Others will be political, while others will be religious; some will be concerned with the protection of civil freedoms; some will be attacking a major organisation that they believe has wronged them; and some will be attempting to save the world from humanity's extinction. Whatever their motivation, hacktivists will almost always target prominent websites, typically defacing or replacing the organization's 'landing' pages with their own interpretations of the 'truth.' Because hacktivists rarely target individuals and aren't usually motivated by thievery, they pose little of a threat to us as individuals, unless we work in a laboratory that conducts experimentation on live animals, or in another similarly contentious field. To organisations, however, they constitute a tremendous annoyance, causing public disgrace and, on rare occasions, financial loss, all of which are very much the hacktivists' primary goals. They usually execute their assaults by exploiting known flaws in internet applications. Once detected, these vulnerabilities are relatively easy to fix, but in the meanwhile, they believe that their point has been made if they have received enough exposure. A limited number of hacktivists are only interested in causing havoc and are less concerned with conveying a message; rather, they have discovered a vulnerability and deface a website to demonstrate their prowess. Some hacktivist attacks, such as those carried out by the Anonymous organisation, have a far bigger visibility.

Lone wolves are frequently inexperienced hackers. They frequently start out as skiddies, learning rudimentary hacking skills from online chatrooms and blogs, downloading malware, and attempting to assault progressively high-profile websites. Their aim is usually to acquire accolades from their peers, but it might also be to cause some havoc, and this type of lone wolf can progress from small hacking to minor criminality or hacktivism. Another, more benign sort of lone wolf is driven solely by curiosity, and is more akin to the original hacking group, which was interested in learning how things functioned and improving them if possible. A security specialist or penetration tester is a common career path for this type of hacker. Investigative journalists are a fascinating bunch of people. While their intentions may be good, they frequently use deception to achieve their objectives. Hacking into the voice mails of celebrities, politicians, and others has been one method of illegal interception. It's easy to envision a journalist willing to unlawfully access someone's voicemail being wanting to illegally access someone's computing device, email messages, or internet browsing records, whether they did so directly or through a proxy - that is, paying a hacker to handle the technical parts.

Minor criminals are members of a subculture that prefers to target individuals and small companies over large organisations. Theft of money or information is usually their motivation. Some people profit directly from someone else's bank account or by abusing their credit card. Others may just upload copies of software, music, or movies to torrent sites for others to download for free. Naturally, the pirated material's copyright owner suffers a financial loss as a result of this. Minor criminals can either become huge criminals, particularly if their expertise attracts the attention of organised crime, or they can become respectable security experts. Their decision is sometimes influenced by the amount of money they can make and the likelihood of being caught. Organized criminals, on the other hand, are more sinister. Although instances have been documented in the media when recognised organised criminal gangs have committed cyber-attacks on behalf of terrorist groups or nation states in order to mask their true identities, this group is almost entirely driven by financial gain. Threat actors (as opposed to threat sponsors) will occasionally act in their own best interests and reap the full benefits of their actions. At other times, they'll be acting on behalf of others, who will pay a predetermined price or a percentage of the 'take' in exchange for carrying out the cyber-attack. Organized criminals may frequently acquire information like as lists of valid credit card names and numbers for use in large financial scams or will assign a specific mission to the threat actor in order to obtain valuable information that can subsequently be sold to the highest bidder. Terrorist organisations frequently deploy cyber-attacks for a variety of purposes. The first is to establish or strengthen a position, such as a political or religious one — defacement of western websites is a good example of this. The second type is the stealing of funds from organisations in order to advance their ideals and objectives. The third, and potentially more deadly, option is to destroy their political or religious adversaries' infrastructure.

Every country has important infrastructure. Communications, emergency services, energy, financial services, food, government, health, transportation, water, defence, civil nuclear, space, and chemicals are all examples of this. The communications and energy industries, in particular, are prime targets for terrorism, as a successful strike on either of these sectors would bring massive damage to an adversary. Of course, all other industries will be considered useful targets, although the impact may not be noticed as quickly. There is a nexus here between cyber-attacks carried out by terrorist groups and those carried out by nation states. Cyberattacks by one nation state against another are commonly referred to as "cyber warfare."

We must now consider attackers who launch cyber-attacks from within traditional businesses. One of the most serious risks comes from those currently working for the company. Many of the cyber mishaps they cause are inadvertent, the result of a lack of understanding or deliberate disregard for the risks. It's possible that someone merely clicked on a virus link in an email. Others are more intentional behaviours, such as when an insider duplicates and then steals corporate knowledge that is valuable to a competitor or criminal organisation. Security education, awareness, and training are the most effective ways to cope with inadvertent insider occurrences. Active monitoring of user accounts, internet access, and the use of intrusion detection software will detect some deliberate insider activity in the case of deliberate insider cyber security assaults, but organisations may never be guaranteed of totally preventing insider cyber security attacks. An insider who has been well-trained and put expressly within the organisation to inflict loss or harm is likely to be fully aware of the organization's skills in recognising prospective attackers and will act in a manner that does not raise suspicion.

Security agencies are generally regarded as beneficial. However, because security organisations have the potential to intercept our communications at multiple points, there is significant question about whether they operate totally within the law. GCHQ monitors satellite and fibre-optic cable transmissions on a regular basis, and the resulting intelligence is shared with the NSA via their 'special' connection. It's logical to believe that the NSA conducts similar types of surveillance and that the results are shared in a 'quid pro quo' arrangement. Let us not forget, however, that the primary job of security services is to help the police and military while also protecting the country from cyber threats, terrorism, severe crime, and espionage.

Motivations, Means & Methodology

Cyberattacks are carried out for a variety of reasons by different attackers. Many, if not all, cyber-attackers are motivated by the potential of financial gain from 'easy' money, which allows them to live a lavish lifestyle or to fund activities that are harmful to the public good, such as crime or terrorism. Ransom, theft, or fraud can all result in financial gain. Ransomware assaults are becoming more common. The prevalence of ransomware has been steadily rising. All an attacker needs to do is get access to a victim's computer, which is commonly done through an email scam in which the user either clicks on a link to a malicious website or unintentionally runs an application disguised as part of the email. Theft is divided into two distinct categories. The first occurs when the target's banking or credit card credentials are stolen, and the second occurs when these data are used to purchase goods or services, with the legitimate owners of the money being forced to part with it. As part of a bigger scheme, the credentials could be sold to other thieves. Fraud induces people to part with their money willingly in exchange for little or nothing. Cyber fraud frequently advertises the sale of pricey computer software at a discount. The software could be ineffective, difficult to register, or include malware. More damaging is fraud targeting someone at the executive level, in which someone with financial sign-off rights at the CEO's company is duped into authorising funds to be transferred to the attacker, who may use phishing techniques to gain access to the CEO's email account or may email an employee from an email domain name that closely resembles the target company's true domain name.

Revenge or purposeful harm can be very aggravating. Some cyber-attacks are carried out in response to a victim's action, or what the victim perceives to be an action. The conduct may have been completely justified, but the attacker believes they have suffered some form of hurt, deprivation, or harm as a result of the action and concludes that a cyber retaliation is necessary. For example, this could be a disgruntled ex-employee. The consequences of revenge or malicious harm attacks may be catastrophic, and many careers have been nearly lost as a result of the claims and charges made during the attack, whether real or untrue. Attacks of this nature can land the perpetrator in legal hot water, especially if libel suits are filed, or if the material they post is judged defamatory, racist, homophobic, or falls into any of a number of other prohibited categories. These attacks are usually one person against another, one person against an organisation, or a group of people against an organisation.

Espionage has been included because, whatever its aim, it inevitably entails some type of cyber-attack in the context of cyber security, and regardless of who the attackers are on, the 'other' side will perceive them as hostile. One must believe that the security services are well-versed in cyber espionage, and that identifying and tracking down criminals and terrorists is just as important to them as learning about the enemy's objectives and capabilities.

There's also a distinction between corporate or industrial espionage, which is done to obtain an economic or other advantage over another company; legitimate surveillance by the police and security agencies; and, ultimately, espionage by one country against another. However, espionage is a difficult subject for many people because it violates our need for privacy, and while we are generally satisfied that the security services are acting in our best interests, we are concerned that our privacy is being invaded, whether it is or not. Cyber espionage is either commercial or state-sponsored.

Music, filmmaking, equations, industrial processes, software, designs, and development are only few of the domains where intellectual property is stolen. Industrial espionage has existed for many years. Organizations continue to lose intellectual property due to a combination of weak security and an inability to react quickly enough to new technology.

Investigative journalism is another field. The press frequently succeeds in persuading governments that extra regulation of investigative journalism is unnecessary and that self-regulation is sufficient. This may be accurate, and if an investigation is truly 'in the public interest,' there will be little or no opposition from those who are being investigated. The press, on the other hand, is known for overstepping its bounds, becoming intrusive, and causing considerable misery to innocent individuals. While breaking into a celebrity's voicemail may not be difficult, it frequently results in gossip rather than serious misconduct.

Few people would have equated whistleblowing with cyber security until lately. That was changed by Edward Snowden. Snowden, who had been working as a contractor for the National Security Agency, revealed to three journalists that the NSA had been conducting widespread surveillance programmes on its own citizens. This includes data from some of the greatest technology corporations in the United States, as well as data gathered from worldwide telephone networks and the internet to collect information on millions of Americans. Snowden also claimed that the UK's GCHQ has gathered, stored, and analysed massive amounts of personal data from worldwide email messages, phone calls, and other sources. This, according to Snowden, is "perhaps the most invasive intercept system in the world." Governments on both sides of the Atlantic began making quick legislative modifications to either make some of their actions lawful, or to wrap their more evil acts in such legal verbiage that they look to be legitimate, while allowing for enough 'interpretation.' Whistle-blowers must be fully committed to their cause, fully aware that, while the information they provide may be morally or legally reprehensible, the state will almost certainly find a way to portray them as criminals, and they will almost certainly be punished for doing what they and many others believe is morally correct.

Security experts should be aware of the methods that a hacker might use to target an individual or an organisation. A short internet search for the term 'hacking tools' yields millions of results, thus it should come as no surprise that there is a software programme that can accomplish practically any goal. Many of these tools are free to download, while others may require payment in the form of a one-time cost or a membership. Hackers, particularly those with strong coding skills, are becoming more commercially conscious.

The low cost and widespread availability of these tools are only one side of the coin; the other is that they are becoming much easier to use, so it is easy to see how almost anyone with a little motivation can mount a cyber-attack, often with little understanding of the damage they may cause or the depth of trouble they may find themselves in. More experienced attackers will have a thorough understanding of both the tools and the potential outcomes and will plan accordingly.

We should also look at how attackers carry out cyber-attacks and the tools they use to accomplish their goals. Cyber-attacks can appear to be random occurrences; they are frequently untargeted attacks in which the attacker uses a scattergun strategy to impact as many targets as possible. This type of attack may necessitate some preliminary inquiry, but it is more likely to be the consequence of the acquisition of an email address list or a credit card user list. The resources or tools needed to carry out this type of attack are almost probably 'commodity' resources that may be discovered or purchased from online sources.

A different form of attack is perpetrated by more organised individuals or groups, and it is frequently directed at specific persons, groups of individuals, or organisations. Some of the resources or tools required to carry out this type of attack will almost certainly be of the 'commodity' type mentioned above, but in cases where specialist attackers have been hired, the tools will almost certainly form a bespoke payload, and may be individually crafted or modified for that specific attack. It would be unusual for an attacker to employ only one tool to carry out a more comprehensive cyber-attack. It's far more likely that they'll employ a variety of tools, each tailored to carry out a different aspect of the larger plan; these are known as 'blended' attacks.

While the stages of an attack may differ, a sophisticated cyber-attack will usually take a highly structured shape, such as Lockheed Martin's 'Cyber Kill Chain' model. There are several stages:

1. Reconnaissance is the first step. The attacker will conduct a reconnaissance of the target's networks and systems in the first stage, seeking for known vulnerabilities that can be exploited as a means of entrance. Because it must accomplish its goals without alerting an intrusion detection system, this reconnaissance is likely to be highly complex.

2. Weaponisation comes next. The attacker will prepare the software tools needed to achieve the objectives after surveying the target and understanding the particular objectives. This may entail modifying current commodity tools or, in extreme circumstances, developing bespoke specialised tools. Attackers may also use this moment to gain network or system access, at least until the payload has been released and tested.

3. Delivery is the next step. The attacker will now upload the tools to the target system or systems, or to a specific user, making sure they are hidden from plain sight as well as detection by more sophisticated ways. Loading malware onto a USB memory stick that will be found by or handed to a user, attaching malware to an email, posting it on a social media website, or posting it on a 'watering hole' website are all possibilities.

4. Exploitation of weakness. In order to execute the malware, the attacker must be certain that the final attack will be successful, hence a known weakness on the target machine will be exploited. A user could also do this by clicking on a link or opening an email attachment.

5. Installation of malware. The attacker will now install the malware after gaining access to the target system or systems. The malware suite will frequently include additional code to prevent it from being uninstalled by accident, and it may also be time-stamped by the attacker to appear to be compatible with other legitimate operating systems or application software.

6. Command and control. After ensuring that the tools will function as intended, the actual attack can be carried out by either selecting the most appropriate time, such as when many of the security support workers are not at work, or staging a large distraction to divert attention away from the real attack. To do so, the attacker could employ an internet channel, DNS, or email protocols.

7. Goal-oriented actions. The attacker can get down to business, harvesting user credentials, escalating privileges to get access to systems that were previously out of reach, exfiltrating other data, or simply modifying, deleting, or destroying systems.

The Lockheed Martin Cyber Kill Chain hypothesis states that if the defensive organisation understands the sort of attack, they may halt it at any of the earlier phases with the correct tools and procedures, preventing the attacker from accomplishing their final goals. This, however, assumes that the defending organisation can either outrun the attacker or at the very least keep up with the onslaught. In some extreme instances, two successive attacks will be carried out: the first to determine the precise specifics of the target, and the second to carry out the actual attack. The entire process can take many months, especially if there is a lot of custom software to design and test.

For commodity-type attacks, a simpler approach would be used, in which no additional software development is required, and the payload is deployed and the attack is executed very quickly after initial reconnaissance, in order to take advantage of the element of surprise, which may be lost if the time interval is too great.

There are numerous cyber-attack avenues available. Dark patterns demonstrate what may be accomplished while staying just on the legal side of the law. Dark patterns are totally legal (but frequently immoral) techniques employed by website designers to entice the unsuspecting into making a decision or choices that they would not ordinarily make. Disguising buttons and tricking users into installing malware are examples of bait and switch tactics. Clicking on what looks to be a valid weblink and being directed to a virus site are examples of disguised advertisements. Enforced subscriptions, in which the user discovers that they have signed up for an ongoing subscription rather than a one-time purchase. The only way out is to call the organization's helpline, which will cost you a premium rate call. Friend spam is when you register your email, Facebook, or Twitter account with a website, and the website then publishes content or sends mass email, Facebook messages, or Twitter messages using your account. Dark patterns are a classic example of hidden costs. The user begins to make a purchase on a website, but when it comes time to pay, they discover that other expenses have been imposed, such as processing fees, taxes, and so on. The fees may be valid, but they have been subtracted from the original stated price to make it appear more appealing. Misdirection strategies are used to boost website income. Customers are encouraged to input additional order information on several well-known company websites. The website then adds more products to the overall cost, and the only way to remove them is through menu options that are cleverly hidden. Users are either not allowed to copy and paste details from a supplier's website to discourage them from finding a better price, or the organisation refuses to allow its products to display on price comparison websites, arguing that this gives the shopper a better value. Roadblocks are commonly used to keep users from proceeding with a transaction until they have agreed to something. Bypassing this type of dark pattern typically necessitates a significant amount of work. Basket extras are goods in a user's online shopping basket that have had their price change unexpectedly. While you go to buy a membership, you may notice that the website has changed your selection to a three-year package, when a one-year subscription is actually better value for money. This style of dark pattern might also include other things in a user's internet purchasing basket without their knowledge, such as insurance.

When firewall ports are left open for an attacker to utilise as a means of entry, application layer attacks occur. Unfortunately, in order for a company to conduct business, at least two ports (port 80 Hypertext Transfer Protocol (HTTP) and port 443 Hypertext Transfer Protocol Secure (HTTPS)) must be open at all times for general internet traffic, and two more ports (port 25 Simple Mail Transfer Protocol (SMTP) and port 445 used by Microsoft services) must be open for email traffic. A cyber-attacker can use this and other ports to target specific applications, such as a web server application, and exploit a known vulnerability.

Botnets allow cyber thieves to target a wide number of potential victims, the vast majority of whom are virtually definitely unwitting recipients. Botnets are made up of a huge number of malware-infected machines, dubbed "zombies," that deliver the payload, which could be spam email or a DDoS attack. The botnet owner, also known as a 'herder,' will have gotten access to these computers at some point, most often by the user clicking on a link in a spam email or a link on a web page, both of which will have downloaded malware onto the user's computer without their knowledge. Using one or a group of command and control computers, the botnet owner will be able to take control of the computer whenever they want. The botnet owner may not use the botnet personally, but he or she may sell the service to individuals or businesses who want to send spam email or launch DDoS assaults without having to build their own botnet. However, it's critical to distinguish between botnets, which are a more aggressive form of cyber-attack, and distributed computing, which involves multiple computers working together in a coordinated research effort. Occasionally, though, law enforcement authorities are able to locate the botnet's command and control servers and shut it down completely.

Brute force attacks are when a cyber-attacker tries every conceivable combination of characters until the proper password is exposed, such as a password. Brute force attacks can take a long time to succeed, but they will always yield the correct result in the end. Although better distributed and parallel computers will minimise the time required, it is still a time-consuming operation, and it is often more efficient to try to uncover a password through other ways, such as social engineering.

Buffer overflow attacks are a tried-and-true method of breaking an application by flooding it with more data than the designer intended. For example, if an application recommends using a username of up to 20 alpha-numeric characters and the user enters 21, the application may enter an unknown state unless the programmer has implemented a check to delete the input if the total exceeds 20 characters. One approach of deploying malware is to conceal it in this type of user input. Once an application has been compromised in this fashion, a cyber-attacker may be able to use the application's features as if he were a legitimate user. Most recently produced software accounts for buffer overflows, but every now and then a new one emerges, giving cyber-attackers a field day until a remedy is discovered and installed.

The injection attack, whereby attackers either inject software code into a programme or otherwise insert banned characters that may cause an application to terminate, leaving access open for the attacker, is another type of attack. In order to execute SQL instructions in Structured Query Language (SQL) databases, one approach is to inject a '&' character.

Another attack vector is network protocol attacks. The protocols that support the internet are insecure. The following protocols are among them:

- Request for Comments (RFC) 768 defines the User Datagram Protocol (UDP)29.
- The Internet Protocol (IP), which was first described in RFC 791;
- TCP (Transmission Control Protocol), which was first described in RFC 793;
- NTP (Network Time Protocol), which was first described in RFC 1305;
- RFC 2460, which defines Internet Protocol Version 6 (IPv6)33;
- RFC 1654 was the first to define BGP34.

There is no need for the reader to grasp how these work in detail; suffice it to say that attackers who can subvert any of them (and a few others) can cause significant damage.

Rogue updates are one of the most common types of cyber-attacks. They frequently prey on unwary or inexperienced users by implying – usually by email or a pop-up on a website – that some aspect of the user's machine is out of date and requires immediate updating. This might be an operating system or a regularly used application, and it will almost certainly result in the machine becoming infected with malware or ransomware.

Because many usernames can be easily guessed by simple software that combines known first names with known surnames, places a full stop between them, and adds '@' and a known email provider's domain name, such as 'john.smith@gmail. com,' email-borne attacks are a very common vector for conducting cyber-attacks.

Such email address lists may be generated fast using software, and emails sent to these addresses can be delivered for little or no cost to the cyber-attacker, possibly reaching thousands of email users with a single click. Spammers rely on people's receptivity to excellent offers, and the virus, ransomware, or other message contained in these emails will invariably result in some successes.

Wi-Fi attacks are fairly widespread, and they often take one of two forms. The more challenging technique is for an attacker to intercept a wireless access point's signal, store the intercepted data, and then use 'brute force' searching to obtain the access key. WEP or WPA-only access points will be considerably easier to hack into than WPA2-enabled access points. The second (and frequently simpler) technique is for the cyber-attacker to set up his own access point with an SSID that is similar to or identical to that of a legitimate access point, such as in any public location that offers 'free' Wi-Fi. When an unwary user attempts to join and provides their access key, the attacker's computer captures the information and allows him to access the real network as if he were a legitimate user. In addition, if the attacker is clever enough, he will allow the user's computer to connect to the real network, resulting in a 'man-in-the-middle' attack. He may now track the user's application login credentials, granting him access to at least one system within the company, from which he may be able to access additional systems or even discover he has administrative privileges.

End-user devices that have their Bluetooth wireless connection activated and may be intercepted and accessed from the attacker's device are the target of Bluetooth-based attacks. These usually don't lead to complete network access, and if the attacker is after a specific user, Bluetooth is a great approach to accomplish his goals. An attacker can acquire access to the victim's address book, calendar, email, and much more over Bluetooth. The instance of Dublin Airport, which exploits a passenger's Bluetooth identity to track them as they pass through the airport, is an example of Bluetooth misuse.

Because cellular networks use a substantially more complex key management and encryption method to safeguard the device and its data, cyber-attacks against cellular mobile devices such as smartphones and tablet computers will largely use Wi-Fi or Bluetooth as a technique for attacking the device.

Social media-based attacks are extremely common. These frequently entail the collection of personally identifiable information or the enticement of users to visit watering holes. Attackers are highly interested in obtaining personally identifiable information (PII). People who use social networking sites like Facebook, Twitter, and LinkedIn routinely supply large amounts of personal information, which might be exploited by a cyber-attacker to obtain access not only to the individual's social media account, but also to their bank accounts and other websites. It's also problematic when people's friends, acquaintances, and co-workers share information about them on social media, often without considering the ramifications. Many companies are increasingly searching for prospective workers' social media profiles in order to do covert background checks. An attacker who wants to learn the names of corporate directors can do so for free on the Company's House website. Many people are taken aback when they are enticed with a watering hole (gift or prize). Once a cyber-attacker has identified a possible target on a social media site, they can entice them to visit a malware-infected website known as a 'watering hole.' For example, messages on social media promising the chance to win an iPad. These lead to malware sites, which can lead to the disclosure of additional personal information as well as the installation of a virus on the computer.

Social engineering is almost always a low-tech way for a cyber-attacker to obtain personally identifiable information or gain unauthorised access to a computer. This can often start with a simple phone call or email, with the goal of tempting or inviting the individual to provide information or click on a link to a malware website, as in the watering hole example above. An engineer tracing an issue or wanting to check the gas/electricity metre; a person posing as someone from the IT department, frequently over the phone; or a 'contractor' attempting to talk their way past the reception desk are all examples of social engineering. People proficient in sweet talking the user, seeming to be attempting to help (especially elderly or less technically savvy users), and proposing to make their computers more safe or work more rapidly, are responsible for much social engineering. The user's PC is frequently infected with malware or ransomware as a result of these types of calls.

Data aggregation does not constitute a cyber-attack in and of itself. It is essentially a method of combining facts or information about an individual or a group of individuals in order to create a more thorough image of them in order to exploit them in some way, as explained in previous chapters. When paired with the different cyber-attack tactics discussed here, aggregating the generated data becomes a very strong tool in an attacker's hands.

Those conducting cyber attacks must think about the risks, and the Security Specialist's job is to raise the stakes. The risk of being found applies equally to cyber-attacks as it does to normal behaviour. The consequences of being identified as the perpetrator of a cyber-attack vary depending on the type of attacker. Some will cause the miscreant little more than public embarrassment; others may result in imprisonment or an international incident. The attacker's technical talents and attention to detail will influence the likelihood of being detected. Inexperienced cyber criminals are more likely to make basic errors in their methods, whereas a more mature or experienced attacker, or a state-sponsored group, is almost certain to launch a highly professional, potentially multi-part attack.

To make it more difficult for attackers and increase their risk, security experts must implement sufficient controls. In a cyber-equivalent of a cost-benefit analysis, the cyber-attacker will weigh the risks against the potential advantages of success and make an informed decision on whether or not to proceed. Government agencies in the United States have been known to demand the extradition of alleged criminals whose networks and systems have been hacked, albeit inadvertently. This sends a clear message that unless you're a proficient cyber attacker, you shouldn't meddle with government or military organisations unless you're willing to risk major penalties.

SECTION 4:

SECURITY IMPROVEMENT

Infosec Leadership

In the age of digital transformation, cybersecurity approaches to defend against cyber threat attacks on systems and networks demand intelligent risk management to balance limited available resources with the requirement to secure organisations from ever-evolving cyber threat attacks occurrences. Cybersecurity issues, on the other hand, are complicated and cannot be tackled in a one-dimensional manner. As a result, becoming a cybersecurity leader necessitates multi-dimensional and transdisciplinary knowledge. The reason for this is that a cybersecurity leader must understand and control an organization's business plan as well as its vulnerabilities in the face of cyber threat strikes. Risk management and strategic prioritising of cybersecurity tool and cybersecurity defence team expenditures are critical components of such a strategy. As a result, cybersecurity leaders concentrate on ways to fight against cyber assaults. As a result, a well-balanced cybersecurity implementation boosts productivity and innovation in businesses. As a result, cybersecurity leadership is a business discipline, because senior executives must see technology as an integral part of their operations.

Digital transformation processes are driving today's economy and culture, resulting in a new world built on software. Software updates will include new capabilities to do new things, as well as a transformation of core functions or things. This poses a significant obstacle for digital technologies, necessitating competencies in cybersecurity and digital assets in order to transform digital technologies into an organisational change. This necessitates leadership competencies, which include decision-making competencies, diversity of competencies combining young and senior people, ethical competences, organisational competencies, and technological competencies. This improves risk management, makes choices faster, and allows security leadership to spend less time on Cyber threat assault situations that are more likely to be innocuous, unrelated to the business, or for which security safeguards already exist.

Information security leadership must be able to assess technological organisational risks, such as emerging threats and "unknown unknowns" that may affect a company. Following that, they must determine the best cyber threat assault security solutions to mitigate the dangers. Then they must explain the danger to the organization's top management in order to justify defensive spending.

Threat intelligence methods can be a valuable resource for all of these action items, providing information on emerging issues such as which cyber threat attacks are growing more common. We can then figure out which types of cyber-threat attacks are the most expensive for the company being attacked. We can determine what new types of cyber-attackers are emerging, as well as the assets and organisations they are pursuing. We can investigate which security techniques and technology have shown to be the most effective in preventing or reducing specific cyber threat attacks.

With this data, obtained from a number of external data sources, security decision makers can get a comprehensive perspective of the cyber risk environment and the highest risk potential that could affect their company. In this regard, information security leadership may be attained by referring to the key basic areas where threat intelligence aids cybersecurity leaders in making sound decisions.

With the flood of data generated by the digital transformation and its impact on the transformation process, digitisation has become a key concern for businesses. However, the present dynamics of digital change make digital business development a never-ending endeavour. As a result, digital masters will combine this massive amount of data with the most recent innovations in Artificial Intelligence, Machine Learning, Internet of Things, Big Data and Analytics, and other fields, and use the resulting insights to make smarter decisions, see the future more clearly, and eliminate inefficiencies in digital businesses and organisational development. As a result, to establish future-proof digital business strategies, design structures, marketing concepts, and data and process security concepts for public and private organisations, a digital master must grasp digital upheavals and innovations. As a result, digital masters must combine digital and leadership qualities to achieve performance beyond what either dimension can provide on its own. As a result, digital capabilities make it easier and less dangerous for digital masters to launch new digital initiatives, while also offering revenue leverage to alter digital company. Despite the fact that digital capabilities support a focus on an organization's uniqueness, a digital master's plan aimed at cross-company digital business development should add value and competitiveness to this uniqueness. As a result, digital masters rely on data-driven insights to make decisions on how to proceed in order to maximise productivity. This necessitates the creation of a governance architecture with appropriate committees that meets the demands of the organisation. On this foundation, a governance model that meets the organization's core needs can be developed. The phases preceding that, on the other hand, necessitate selecting how to enhance the organization's digital leadership/mastering capabilities, which are critical to innovation and long-term value development. This is built on a ground-breaking template for public and private sector business models to embrace the digital transformation wave.

Risk Management

Risk management must be done openly and transparently by Infosec specialists at a senior level. We must recognise and acknowledge danger as a reality. Denying its existence, significance, or likelihood just serves to spread ignorance rather than informed decision-making. Security risks exploit a vulnerability in an asset, resulting in a negative impact. They also combine with the presence of a vulnerability to give us with the possibility or probability of the threat being carried out when there is motivation. Impacts and likelihood are then combined to yield risk.

However, there are two sides to the topic of motivation: on the one hand, there are attackers who have a strong motivation for carrying out the attack, and on the other hand, there are script kiddies who stumble into an exploit and try it out to see what happens. When either situation is combined with a vulnerability, the risk increases dramatically. People frequently mix up the terms threats and risks. They can say there's a chance of rain when they really mean there's a chance of rain. The danger is that if it does rain, we will be soaked. The distinction is small, but significant when it comes to risk management, as we'll see later.

It's also pretty uncommon for folks to mix up likelihood and probability. There is a significant difference between both, with probability being an objective evaluation with some type of statistical backing and likelihood being subjective, based on emotions and gut feeling. Many aspects of cyber security have so-called "inherent" risks, the most serious of which is the chance that, despite all attempts to defend the organisation, an attacker may still be able to gain access to a system and do damage.

Assets can be nearly anything in general, but in the context of cyber security, they can comprise not just the data - the information we're attempting to secure but also the entire technological infrastructure – hardware, software, data and information, HVAC, and premises. Last but not least, there are the personnel with the technical knowledge and skills needed to create and execute suitable security measures, as well as maintain and respond to occurrences.

Although I have drawn a distinction between data and information, I have used the terms interchangeably in this book because they are both assets with value for their owners that must be equally protected, even if the owner of the original data and the owner of the resulting information may be completely different entities.

Vulnerabilities are things that make securing assets less effective, and they occur in two types. Extrinsic vulnerabilities are those that are poorly applied, such as software that is out of date due to a lack of patching or vulnerable due to poor coding practises. Intrinsic vulnerabilities are those that are inherent in the very nature of an asset, such as the ease of erasing information from magnetic media (whether accidentally or deliberately), whereas extrinsic vulnerabilities are those that are poorly applied.

Threats take use of weaknesses to harm an asset whether it is copied or stolen (confidentiality), changed or damaged (integrity), or access is denied (availability). Vulnerabilities can exist even if we are unaware of them. A hacker may have identified security flaws in an operating system or application that the software vendor is unaware of, this type of vulnerability is known as a zero-day vulnerability.

One of the most serious issues with this type of vulnerability is that once it is discovered, it will be relentlessly abused until a fix is found and, more crucially, implemented. When a software vendor offers a fix, awareness of the vulnerability grows even further, which typically leads to a rise in attacks. There's also the potential that individuals and organisations will fail to implement the fix, putting themselves at greater risk. The situation in which attackers reverse engineer known vulnerabilities in order to design and build specialised attack tools is an interesting twist on the release of known vulnerabilities.

Other flaws are more evident, such as a lack of antivirus software, which can allow malware to reach a target via email, or a lack of firewall protection, which can cause the same issues with internet access. Disgruntled employees can either reconfigure the organization's defences to allow malware through, or entirely circumvent them by putting malware on a USB stick, for example. Computers without passwords, operating system and application software with default passwords, and shared passwords are easy targets for even the most inexperienced attacker. Improving cyber security by removing or minimising vulnerabilities will go a long way.

The risk likelihood is the probability of something happening. The term "likelihood" is a fairly subjective one. It may rain if there are dark clouds in the sky, but it may not. All we can say is that there is a chance of rain, and depending on the amount of cloud, we may believe that the chance of rain is greater or lesser. It is not a particularly scientific form of weather prediction, but it does give

On the other hand, probability is a far more objective concept. Probability is based on evidence, usually statistical data that can help us make decisions, and it is frequently expressed in percentage terms. Again, it may be erroneous or expressed with a margin of error, but probability at the very least has a better scientific foundation. Probability is sometimes referred to as a qualitative assessment, while likelihood is sometimes referred to as a quantitative assessment.

The challenge we confront in risk management is determining one of the two types of measures to use: subjective likelihood assessment or objective probability evaluation. Indeed, combining the two is a frequent method, for example, using numerical ranges to improve the subjective aspect of both impact and likelihood.

Impact scales				
Level of impact	Operational	Financial	Legal and regulatory	Reputational
Very low	Partial loss of a single service	Loss of less than £25K	Warning from regulatory body	Minor negative publicity
Low	Total loss of a single service	Loss between £25K and £250K	Penalties up to £10K	Local negative publicity
Medium	Partial loss of multiple services	Loss between £250K and £1M	Penalties between £10K and £50K	National negative publicity
High	Total loss of multiple services	Loss between £1M and £25M	Penalties between £50K and £500K	EU-wide negative publicity
Very high	Total loss of all services	Loss exceeds £25M	Penalties exceed £500K	Worldwide negative publicity

Although we have provided boundaries for the levels, there will be a degree of uncertainty about the upper and lower limits of each, but in general the ranges should be sufficient to provide a fairly accurate assessment. Clearly these ranges will differ from one scenario to another but set a common frame of reference when there are a substantial number of assessments to be carried out.

The typical risk management process involves taking a focus on context establishment, risk assessment and risk treatment. There are also steps thereafter on communication and consultation as well as monitoring and review stages. These latter steps are key constantly building up controls and further mitigating risks but for the purposes of this book we focus on the former.

Likelihood scales			
Level of likelihood	Hacking, malware and social engineering	Environmental	Errors, failures, misuse and physical
Very unlikely	The event is likely to occur once a week	The event is likely to occur once a decade	The event is likely to occur once a month
Unlikely	The event is likely to occur once a day	The event is likely to occur once a year	The event is likely to occur once a week
Possible	The event is likely to occur several times a day	The event is likely to occur once a month	The event is likely to occur once a day
Likely	The event is likely to occur several times an hour	The event is likely to occur weekly	The event is likely to occur several times a day
Very likely	The event is likely to occur at any time	The event is likely to occur at any time	The event is likely to occur at any time

Let's have a look at how to create a context. We can certainly make some kind of assessment if we merely look at the basic components of risk as mentioned above, but any judgement will be made in isolation unless it is placed inside the framework in which the organisation operates. The first phase in the risk management process is to understand the context in which the organisation operates, such as financial, commercial, and political factors, so that subsequent processes can take these factors into consideration when deciding how to treat risks.

After that, we'll look at risk assessment. The risk management process's second stage is divided into three parts: risk identification, risk analysis, and risk evaluation.

The ability to identify risks is critical. Risk management starts with identifying assets, determining their value to the organisation, and calculating the impact if they are destroyed or lost. Even if the asset is shared among several divisions in an organisation, all assets require a single clearly defined owner who will have overall accountability for the item. Some organisations assign ownership of information assets to the IT department, which is a mistake (unless the asset is IT-specific), because the IT department can easily become the unwitting owner of many assets over which they have little or no control, despite the assets being stored on the IT department's systems, because only the genuine owner of the asset can estimate its value to the organisation. After we've established the assets, their ownership, and their worth to the organisation, we can continue on to figuring out what can harm them and what (if any) vulnerabilities they have, which gives us a starting point for determining the possibility or probability. It is critical that we examine the impact of asset loss or degradation, as well as the vulnerabilities that may contribute to this, the threats that these assets face, and the possibility that the threats will exploit the vulnerabilities and cause an impact.

When assessing dangers, we can use a variety of models, one of which is known by the abbreviation D.R.E.A.D. and generates the following questions:

- Damage (We ask how severe an attack be?)
- Reproducibility (We ask how easy it would be to reproduce the attack?)
- Exploitability (We ask how much work would be required to launch the attack?)
- Affected users (We ask how many people will be impacted?)
- Discoverability (We ask how easy it would be to discover the threat?)
- Although subjective, each question's response is given a numerical value (ranging from 1 to 3), and the aggregate of the five elements determines the relative threat level.

Impact and likelihood are two important outputs that can be determined through qualitative or quantitative impact and likelihood assessments. Quantitative assessment uses objective numerical data, such as financial values for impact and percentages for likelihood, whereas qualitative assessment uses general subjective terms such as low, medium, and high, whereas quantitative assessment uses objective numerical data, such as financial values for impact and percentages for likelihood. Each method has advantages and disadvantages. Qualitative evaluation can be completed fast and does not involve extensive research or investigation, whereas quantitative evaluation takes longer but usually yields more accurate results. It is up to the organisation to decide if such precision adds value to the evaluation process. If the resulting danger is really high, the situation will require immediate action, regardless of whether the risk is 90% or 95%.

In a semi-quantitative assessment, qualitative and quantitative assessments are mixed. For impact assessments, low may suggest a financial value between zero and one million pounds; medium might indicate a financial value between one million and ten million pounds; and high might indicate a financial value greater than ten million pounds. Low may indicate a probability between zero and 35 percent; medium may suggest a probability between 35 percent and 70 percent; and high may indicate a probability greater than 70 percent. This enables for a more accurate risk assessment, which is particularly useful when presenting a business case to the executive board.

Then we can think about risk analysis. We integrate the impact and likelihood in the form of a risk matrix, which allows us to compare risk levels, after we have completed the initial risk identification. A risk matrix is essentially a visual representation of the relative levels of all the hazards we've discovered, which will help us understand the order in which we want to address them, based on some sort of priority system. The most popular risk matrices have three, four, or five value ranges. Three is frequently thought to be too few to be meaningful, whereas five provides for the possibility of having too many results in the centre. Because the assessor must choose a figure on each side of the centre ground, four is sometimes regarded to be a superior choice.

The risk assessor, in collaboration with others, will assign a risk category to each section of the matrix in order to aid prioritisation. Alternatively, each column in the matrix can be given a value, allowing for risk grouping. Risks ranging from 1 to 5 could be classified as trivial; 6 to 10 as minor; 11 to 15 as moderate; 16 to 21 as serious; and 21 to 25 as critical.

Finally, we can consider risk assessment. This is where we decide how we will handle risks, usually by keeping track of the results in a risk register. We have four options in the management of the risk:

- **Termination:** we either quit doing the action that may pose a risk, or we simply avoid doing it if it is a planned activity. While this will usually eliminate the risk completely, it may cause other issues for the organisation. For example, if an organisation was planning to build a data centre and the risk assessment indicated a high likelihood of flooding in the proposed location, the decision would almost certainly be to abandon that location and build elsewhere to avoid the risk. However, this could be an issue because alternate sites may be difficult to find, prohibitively expensive, or have other limitations. As a result, the organisation would have to weigh all of these risks against one another.

- **Transfer:** we have the option of transferring the risk to a third party. This is commonly done through insurance, but it's crucial to realise that even if the organisation shares or bears the risk, they still bear responsibility for it. However, some insurance firms would refuse to insure certain sorts of risks, especially when the entire potential impact is unknown, forcing the organisation to find another way to deal with it.

- **Treatment/Reduction:** We can take steps to lessen the risk's impact or likelihood, which may necessitate reducing the threat or vulnerability where possible. Threats cannot always be eliminated - for example, a criminal attempting to hack into an organization's website cannot be eliminated, but it may be able to lessen the possibility by implementing stringent firewall regulations or other countermeasures.

- **Tolerate:** we can choose to accept or tolerate a danger, particularly if it has a low impact or probability. This is not to be mistaken with ignoring risk, which is never a good idea, but it is done consciously and objectively, and it is reviewed at intervals or whenever a component of the risk changes, such as the asset value, threat level, or vulnerability. Risk acceptance is mostly determined by an organization's risk appetite, or attitude toward risk. Some organisations have a very low risk appetite, such as pharmaceutical businesses, which recognise that failing to keep product information private might result in significant financial loss if they are stolen, or in people dying if the manufacturing process is tampered with.

Then we can think about residual risk. While some types of risk treatment will entirely eliminate the risk, others will invariably leave some residual risk behind. When compared to the cost of the expected damage, this residual risk is either impossible to treat or, more commonly, prohibitively expensive. Residual risk must be accepted by the organisation, and it will need to be monitored and reviewed on a regular basis to avoid becoming a treatable concern.

Risk mitigation is defined as a reduction in the risk's exposure (its impact or consequence) and/or the possibility of it occurring. We go to the final stage of the risk management process; risk treatment and the implementation of controls or countermeasures to carry out our decisions once we have determined on the most appropriate technique of handling risks. Controls are divided into four categories:

- detective controls, which enable us to know or be notified when something has occurred or is now occurring;
- directive controls, which elicit some sort of action that must be carried out;
- preventive controls, which prevent something from happening in the first place;
- corrective controls, which are used to address an issue after it has occurred.

Directive and preventative measures are proactive in nature, since they are implemented prior to an attack to lessen the impact or limit the possibility of it occurring. Detective and remedial controls are reactive in nature, as they are implemented only after an assault has occurred.

The four categories of control are implemented using the following methods:

- Procedural controls, which specify what activities must be taken in a specific circumstance. Users are forced to change their system access passwords at regular periods, which is an example of a procedural control. Staff vetting by the HR department is one example of such restrictions.
- Physical controls, such as installing locks on computer room doors to prevent unauthorised entry, which prevent some type of physical activity.

- Technical controls, such as establishing firewall rules in a network, alter the way some type of hardware or software performs.

Strategic risk treatment controls refer to the risk mitigation options of avoid/terminate, transfer/share, reduce/modify, and accept/tolerate; tactical risk treatment options refer to the four types of control: detective, directive, preventative, and corrective; and operational controls refer to the three methods of implementing the controls be they procedural, physical, and technical.

Although not strictly speaking an information risk topic, organisations have linked the risk management process with a system known as the Plan–Do–Check–Act (PDCA) cycle, also known as the Deming cycle, for many years and for a number of objectives. The PDCA cycle has been widely used as a basic reference framework in a variety of disciplines, including cyber security, information security, information risk management, and business continuity management. The following are the important stages:

- Plan - this is where we set the goals and procedures for achieving the desired outcomes. This translates to understanding the organisation and its setting in the context of cyber security.
- Do - this stage entails putting the plan into action, initially as a means of determining whether or not it was successful. This equates to the execution of the information risk management framework in the context of cyber security.
- Check - this is when we look at the results we have gotten from measurement or observation. This equates to testing, monitoring, and reviewing the framework in the context of cyber security.
- Act - when an incident occurs, we put the validated plans into action and incorporate lessons learned into plan updates. This amounts to continuous enhancement of the framework in the context of cyber security.

Although these are related to risk management in general, any of these approaches can be used to tackle risk in terms of cyber security, because cyber threats can be employed equally well against inadequate processes, a lack of effective physical security, and poor technical security.

Business Continuity Management

Business continuity (BC) considers the entire company, whereas disaster recovery (DR) considers only the IT infrastructure, which is usually a component of a company's business continuity (BC) plan. Despite the fact that business continuity encompasses much more than cyber security, understanding the basic principles is critical for preparing for any cyber security disasters. Similarly, disaster recovery is not solely concerned with cyber security, but it can play a significant role in resolving cyber security concerns. Both business continuity and disaster recovery contribute to cyber security in proactive and reactive ways; the proactive side aims to limit the possibility of a threat or hazard causing a disruption, while the reactive side handles the recovery if one does occur.

The longer a disruption lasts, the more influence it has on the organisation, thus it's important to understand the sort of disruption, its duration and impact, as well as how an organisation handles the crisis.

Incident duration and recovery

Timescale	Seconds	Minutes	Hours	Days	Weeks	Months
Failure type	Glitch	Event	Incident	Crisis	Disaster	Catastrophe
Recovery by	Equipment	Equipment	Operations	Management	Board	Government
Recovery mode	Automatic	Automatic	Process	Improvisation	Ad hoc	Rebuild
Action	Proactive	Proactive	Proactive	Reactive	Reactive	Reactive

Glitches are very brief occurrences that last only a few seconds at most and are frequently caused by temporary power outages or a loss of radio or network transmission. Following most problems, activities normally return to normal as the device self-corrects.

The majority of events are only a few minutes long. The technology they affect, like glitches, is generally self-correcting, but it may require some manual intervention on occasion.

Typically, incidents are thought to last little more than a few hours. They, unlike errors and occurrences, necessitate operational resolution, which usually entails physical intervention following a process. The majority of the strategies for dealing with malfunctions, events, and crises are proactive.

Many times, crises might last several days. Despite the fact that organisations may have plans, protocols, and procedures in place to deal with problems, and that operational staff will carry out the necessary remedial activities, some improvisation may be required. A higher level of management is usually always required to take charge of a crisis, make decisions, and interact with senior management and the media.

Weeks are not uncommon for disasters to last. Operational employees will carry out remedial actions, just as they would in a crisis, while some ad hoc action may be required at this stage, and while a higher management layer will oversee activities, the senior management layer will take ultimate responsibility of the situation.

Catastrophes are the most devastating type of disaster, lasting months or even years. Because their enormity tends to touch many areas, even if individual organisations have their own recovery plans in place, it is likely that local, regional, or even national government will be in charge of the crisis, and that a comprehensive infrastructure rebuilding would be required..

Crises, disasters, and catastrophes all require major reactive activity, and each will require an increasing level of event management competence, notwithstanding any pre-emptive preparation or activities to decrease their impact or possibility. Security professionals must realise that the more time spent on preventive work, the less time will be necessary in the aftermath of a cyber-attack.

Business continuity and disaster recovery share the same fundamental Plan–Do–Check–Act cycle. We carry out the risk assessment (risk identification, risk analysis, and risk evaluation) during the Plan stage; we implement the risk treatment options and assemble the plans during the Do stage; we verify that the plans are fit for purpose by testing and exercising during the Check stage; and finally, we put the plans into practise when a disruption occurs during the Act stage.

The process of risk management, in which we identify the organization's assets, owners, and assets; assess the chance of risks occurring; and combine the two to create a perceived level of risk, is closely tied to putting business continuity into practise. We can then offer strategic, tactical, and operational controls, with the business continuity plan (BCP) being one of the most important components.

BC plans must detail the events that will trigger it, as well as who (or which departments) will be responsible for what actions, how they will be contacted, what actions they will take, how, where, and when they will communicate with senior management and other stakeholders, and how they will determine when business has returned to a pre-determined level of normalcy. Although comprehensive instructions may not always be included in the plan due to the fact that they may alter at any time, they should be referenced in the plan.

Although cyber security is only a small component of the entire business continuity process, it does play an important role in certain elements, particularly when it comes to the continued availability of information and resources. The most evident is disaster recovery of information and communications technology (ICT) systems, in which the systems that are most likely to be harmed require some sort of duplication in order to allow for short-term or even instant recovery.

Rather than being a destination, business continuity is frequently referred to as a journey. It considers the entire organisation rather to just the information technology aspects. However, the general business continuity procedure is particularly applicable to cyber security and can be used to assist a company in establishing a strong position.

Business continuity, according to the Business Continuity Institute (BCI), is "the capacity of an organisation to continue delivering its products or services at acceptable quality levels following a disruptive occurrence." As a twist on the concept of risk management, the BCI has devised a business continuity management life cycle with six areas:

BC policy and programme management involves using the overall organization's business strategy to generate a work plan, with each component being managed as a project.

Training, education, and awareness are all part of integrating BC into the organization's culture.

Analyse the organization's priorities and objectives, as well as its assets, prospective impacts, threats or hazards, and vulnerabilities. A risk assessment can be conducted based on this information, and critical metrics such as the recovery time objective (RTO), the maximum allowable outage (MAO), and the maximum tolerance data loss (MTDL) can be calculated.

Based on the metrics determined during the analysis stage, the business continuity management strategy and approach can now be determined, and decisions can be made about what proactive measures should be implemented, how response to an incident will be organised, and how the organisation will recover to normal operational levels or to a new, revised level of normality.

The proactive and reactive procedures agreed upon in the previous stage will require the efforts of employees from many sectors of the organisation to implement the business continuity response.

Validation which includes exercising, maintaining, and reviewing the various response and recovery plans, is a separate activity from embedding the business continuity culture into the organisation because it deals with the inclusion of people who may have already been involved in the previous stages and who do not require an introduction to the subject; rather, they must be able to exercise, validate, and fine-tune them as needed.

The initial steps will be to respond to the incident by gathering the incident management team, acquiring a better knowledge of the issue, and deciding which parts of the plan will be implemented. It will also be crucial to consider producing a statement that may be presented to the media, customers, and suppliers at this time to manage their expectations.

The developed processes and procedures (which may include disaster recovery methods) will then be put into operation, and depending on the severity of the emergency, this may take some time. If this is the case, it will be necessary to issue additional media statements. Finally, once the crisis has been handled, business can resume normalcy, or a new level of normalcy if the consequences have been severe. All aspects of business continuity are covered by the international standard ISO 22301:2012 – Societal security – Business continuity management systems – Requirements.

The availability defined by the analysis step of the business continuity process is one of the primary features of a business continuity plan. Disaster recovery refers to the process of bringing systems, applications, and services back online after they have failed catastrophically. While this may be true for some services, it is not true for all, because proactive work can (and typically should) be done, and it is possible that only one component of the service has failed, necessitating the use of a disaster recovery method. Disaster recovery, like any other business continuity project, has both proactive and reactive aspects, and because there is no one magic solution, we'll describe some of the choices in broad terms.

There are three types of standby systems to choose from (cold, warm and hot). Because the loss of a data centre or computer room holding both systems would clearly result in no recovery capacity, most well-designed standby operations would ensure that there is an effective physical separation between the active and standby systems. Traditionally, businesses have assumed that a minimum distance of 30 kilometres between data centres is sufficient to ensure that a severe incident impacting one data centre does not affect the other. Systems, as used here, can refer to any system that is engaged in providing the organization's service, including web servers at the front end, back-end servers and support systems, and critical components of the interconnecting networks.

Cold standby systems usually rely on hardware platforms that are used by multiple companies. They may have electricity and an operating system installed, but they are unlikely to have much, if any, user application software installed because to the subtle differences in each organization's requirements. There will be no data loaded as well. This is the least efficient way of data restoration because it can take a long time and effort to load the operating system (if it hasn't previously been done), load and configure user programmes, and restore data from backup media. It will, however, invariably be the most cost-effective alternative for companies that can stomach a lengthier RTO. Another downside of cold standby systems is that if they are shared with other organisations, there may be a resource conflict if more than one organisation declares an incident at the same time, or close to it.

Warm standby systems will typically come pre-loaded with operating systems, some or all user applications, and data up to a specified point of backup. This indicates that the primary goal is to bring the data completely up to date, reducing the amount of time necessary for restoration. Warm standby systems are always more expensive to provide than cold standby systems, so it's usual for companies to use a single warm standby system to provide restoration capabilities for a number of comparable systems to save money. Additionally, organisations that update their application software on a regular basis can use their warm standby systems for training, development, and testing before putting a new or updated application into production.

Hot standby systems come in a variety of flavours, but high availability systems are fast becoming the norm, especially in situations where no downtime can be tolerated at all. A basic hot standby system will be designed to be as close to a warm standby system as possible, with the exception that the data will be completely up to date, necessitating a real-time connection between the active and standby systems. The active system simply transmits data to the standby, but continues processing without waiting for confirmation that the data has been written to disc. The second (and faster) method is known as synchronous working, in which the active system simply transmits data to the standby, but does not wait for confirmation that the data has been written to disc. Synchronous working is the second, slightly slower (but more reliable) mode, in which the active system sends data to the standby and then waits for confirmation that the data has been written to disc before continuing processing. In the first method, there is always the potential that some data may not be received by the standby system, which will be insufficiently robust in circumstances where 100% reliability is required (for example, in financial transactions). Because this method provides 100% reliability at the sacrifice of speed, there will always be a little time lag between transactions in the second method. It will also be more expensive to deploy since very fast transmission circuits – mainly point-to-point optical fibre would be required.

While the focus is often on restoring critical systems, organisations should not forget the networks and communications technology that underpin them. Key elements of the communications network should be replicated whenever possible so that the failure of one does not result in a complete loss of connectivity. Many businesses now use two different transmission providers to ensure that if one experiences a big network outage, the other can still offer service. Of course, if one is functioning as a carrier for the other, a failure of the major provider's network could result in the other losing service as well. Larger companies utilise load balancing systems to distribute the load over multiple servers during peak periods on their websites, and many additionally duplicate their firewall infrastructure for further protection.

Everything revolves around power. The systems and networks would be unable to function without it, and business would grind to a halt very fast. Those businesses that experience frequent power outages are likely to have already invested in a standby generator or, at the very least, an uninterruptible power supply (UPS) system that will keep the lights on for a set period of time. Nowadays, the two are usually integrated, so that a UPS system continues to deliver power and removes any power spikes from the supply, after which the standby generator kicks in and provides power for as long as the fuel supply lasts. Many aspects of disaster recovery are covered under the international standard ISO/IEC 27031:2011 – Information technology – Security approaches – Guidelines for information and communication technology preparation for business continuity.

Access to fire suppression systems can have an impact on a company's capacity to provide services. Without smoke detection and fire-prevention devices, no computer room or data centre would be complete. Very Early Smoke Detection Apparatus (VESDA) systems can detect the emission of smoke (and thus the risk of fire) before it spreads and causes major difficulties. The device operates by pulling air from the surrounding area through pipes and measuring the quality of the air as it passes through a laser detection chamber. A reaction can be triggered if the quality falls below acceptable standards, which is generally the consequence of detection by many detectors. The extinguishing chemical, which is usually an inert gas known as Inergen today, is released into the afflicted area.

Information Security Management – Individuals/SME

Risks must be addressed before they materialise. The first strategy is to take proactive measures to reduce the possibility of an event occurring or to diminish its impact. The other is reactive response, which involves disaster recovery capabilities as well as the hands-on effort of altering system configurations to implement corrective controls after a cyber security issue is discovered. Both methods should lessen the risk, but we may have to accept that some loss or damage will remain. When we leave the house, we make sure the doors and windows are locked. This won't stop a burglar from breaking in, but it will make it more difficult for him. Unless the burglar is deliberately targeting us, there's a good probability he'll move on and try to break into someone else's house.

The same may be said for cyber security. If a determined attacker is sufficiently motivated, skilled, and equipped, he will almost surely be able to acquire access to our data at some point. However, financial restrictions may make repelling him difficult or impossible, therefore the focus should not be on ensuring that he is unable to do so all the time, as this is an unrealistic goal. We should instead aim to make the attacker's task onerous.

We'll start with personal cyber hygiene because it applies to both individuals and people in organisations, and we'll look at the additional procedures that larger organisations can take afterwards. Individual home users, SME users, and users inside bigger organisations can all benefit from the actions mentioned here.

We can look at how to put restrictions in place. Risk management was previously mentioned, and it supplied us with some high-level options:

- Termination, which entails ceasing to do whatever it is that is causing the risk;
- Transfer, in which we share the risk with a third party, usually an insurance company;
- Reduction, in which we identify a means to lessen the likelihood or severity of the assault;
- Tolerance, in which we recognise that some things are beyond our control and that we must live with the consequences.

The majority of the activities we may do in the field of cyber security fall into the third category, risk reduction and it is this area that we will concentrate on the most. There are four broad ways we can go in at the next level:

- detective, in which we put something in place to identify that an attack is underway, such as intrusion detection systems (IDSs) or antivirus software (which will also react to malware it detects);
- preventive, in which we put in place additional facilities to try to prevent an attack from succeeding, such as firewalls;
- directives, such as password policies, in which we lay out policies, processes, and procedures that employees must follow in order to mitigate risk.
- corrective, in which we attempt to repair damage caused by an attack, such as removing infected files and blocking superfluous ports. This orientation is more reactive than the others.

Finally, we get at a position where we may consider the actual controls or countermeasures that we can employ. There are three possibilities:

- physical controls, such as access control systems, that prohibit intruders from getting access to equipment or its surroundings in order to launch a cyberattack or cause other harm;
- technological controls, such as firewalls, that directly address the security of the systems and software that store our data;
- procedural controls, which teach personnel both what not to do and what they must do before, during, and after an attack, and, as previously indicated, may include HR department vetting.

The SANS Institute Sliding Scale for Cyber Security, which provides basic recommendations starting from a proactive position and potentially advancing to a highly reactive one, is worth a brief consideration. Security is integrated and planned into the organization's information architecture, based on the business objectives, at the proactive level. Because the security features of many systems' hardware and software are beyond our control, this is typically the most difficult to do. This is a preventative as well as a directing activity. It continues proactively with passive defence, in which new technology is added to the underlying infrastructure to provide cyber-attack security without the need for human interaction. This is a preventative as well as a detective action.

From here, we proceed into the reactive domain, starting with active defence, in which security personnel respond to occurrences that are beyond the scope of passive defence. This could entail learning everything there is to know about the target, the attack method, and, if possible, the attacker's identity. This is an example of corrective action. A instance in point would be if a company were to be the target of a large-scale DDoS attack. One of the defence measures used in collaboration with the ISP is to redirect the company's internet presence to a different connection and IP address, after which the ISP redirects the DDoS attack to a sink or black hole.

Then we go on to intelligence, where we use the attacker's identify to learn more about them, their motivations, means, and techniques, potentially allowing us to prevent future assaults. This stage of the procedure will necessitate tools for gathering information about the attacker as well as a method for analysing that data to provide useful insight. This, however, may be outside the reach of most businesses, and such an investigation might potentially be carried out by an outside firm with professional InfoSec skills, supporting the attacked company in restoring service. The Diamond Model of Intrusion Analysis is one of the models that makes this study possible.

Finally, we reach the point of reactive offence where we fight back. This course of action is not suggested because it could be dangerous and constitute a cyberattack in and of itself. Individuals and businesses should be discouraged from retaliating in any way; it's far more rational to respond by contacting the proper authorities and leaving offensive retaliation to security and, where applicable, military agencies.

Physical security measures are crucial. If an attacker had physical access to a critical computer system, he could do whatever he wanted by plugging in a USB stick with key-logging software or inserting a CD or DVD containing malware or data from a bogus website. The first step in any proactive activity should always be to restrict physical access to business-critical systems. This means not only keeping bad individuals out of the computer room, but also keeping regular users out unless they have a very clear reason to be there. Access to restricted locations should be the exception rather than the rule, and all access permissions should be granted in accordance with a systematic protocol and evaluated on a regular basis. It is best practise to have a trusted member of staff accompany every visitor to a computer or network equipment room, preferably one of the organization's system administrators. It's worth noting that cleaners aren't immune from this rule. When you have to leave your electronic devices (smartphones, tablet computers, and laptops), you should lock them somewhere secure. When travelling, never leave them unattended in public and keep them hidden from view, especially in crowded places like train stations and airports. Cover our computer camera with a sticky note if we are afraid that it is being accessed by others. If you use a lockable steel security cable to secure a gadget, make sure it's connected to something that can't be readily removed, and keep the key with you.

Online, cyber hygiene is crucial. Users should avoid installing or downloading unfamiliar or unsolicited applications or programmes unless they are certain they are safe and malware-free. No privileged person should utilise an administrator account to download unapproved software in a company setting. Their day-to-day user account should not have the necessary level of access. Users should avoid clicking on links to other pages on a new website unless they are certain they are authentic. Some websites hide the ultimate address by shortening the URL. Allow the mouse pointer to hover over the link before clicking to reveal the true URL.

Many internet activities, such as online shopping, require cookies, but many are annoying and some are detrimental by violating our privacy. Users should review their cookie list on a regular basis and delete those that are no longer needed. The Onion Router (TOR) is a browser that protects users by routing internet traffic through a global network of relays operated by volunteers. It shields one's online actions from prying eyes and stops websites from tracking our physical location. Because it is well recognised for circumventing end-user security protections, such as anti-malware solutions, TOR should not be utilised in a corporate environment. Online forms frequently request information that isn't actually required. Give a response like 'not relevant' if you think the question is superfluous or intrusive. If you don't think they'll need your phone number, for example, enter in 01234 000000 instead. On public computers, users should always remove their browser history. This keeps the next user from discovering any personal information they may have left behind by accident. Junk's also a good idea to delete it on home PCs on a regular basis, as it may take up a lot of disc space. Users should erase temporary internet files on their home computers on a regular basis, as well as whenever they use a public computer, such as one at a library or an internet café. Because different browsers store them in different places, this is always accomplished by opening the security tab in the browser's options. They take up a lot of space on the hard drive and rarely do anything useful. They can be used to track one's web surfing activities in the same way that browser history can. Passwords for the internet should be treated the same manner as passwords for other systems. Later in this chapter, there is a section about user passwords.

The use of social engineering is a strategy by which attackers try to combine their existing knowledge of targeted victim(s) with their social skills like intuition and persuasion to talk their way around the organization's security defences in order to breach cybersecurity

Cold callers who don't know who you are will ask for your credentials. Don't give them anything. Report spam text messages to your network provider if you receive them on your phone. If the message says "Text STOP to unsubscribe," never do so, as this could be a scam to see if the phone belongs to a real person. Don't give in to the need to respond.

Another place where cyber hygiene should be practised is email. Once an attacker gets your email address (or guessed it), they may make you offers of ostensibly appealing goods or services to entice you to click on a link that will almost surely cause you troubles. At best, it will redirect you to a website that sells counterfeit items; at worst, it will install malware on your device that will be used to harvest further data such as banking information, passwords, and other personal information. If an email appears to be suspicious, delete it immediately without examining it. To do so, most email systems allow you to right-click on the message and send it to the trash without any danger. Never respond to emails asking you to provide personal information such as your bank account number, PIN, or password. Banks and credit card providers will never ask you to do this, and even if the email looks like it came from your own bank, it could be a hoax. It's a good idea to cross-reference any suspicious emails with a known-to-be-legitimate one. Spammers, on the other hand, are growing more sophisticated, and it can be difficult to tell the difference between spam and the real thing. If you're not sure, hover your cursor over the URL to make sure it hasn't been obfuscated. Phishing attacks are frequently started by emails that appear to come from a respected financial institution and request that the user verify their online identity. These are almost always hoaxes, and they will direct the naïve user to a bogus website that is virtually identical to the actual one. It is critical not to respond to these, and notifying the legitimate institution whose legitimate website is being misused can be helpful. Spam email is inconvenient. Spam is detected and deleted by email providers' filters without the user's knowledge. If spam email gets past their filter, it may end up in your mail application's spam email folder, making it easy to detect and delete. Do not respond, as this will only notify the sender that they have identified a working email address, and you may receive even more emails as a result. To transfer sensitive information over the internet, use TLS-encrypted email.

It's crucial to backup and restore since it's possible to remove anything valuable by accident, but it's just as easy to make sure you don't. It is not advisable to back up your files to the same hard disc drive that the operating system is installed on; instead, purchase a dependable backup disc drive and utilise the built-in software in Microsoft Windows and Apple operating systems. Consider backing up data to cloud storage like OneDrive as an alternative to a hard disc drive. Always encrypt data while using a backup device such as a memory stick. To avoid unwanted access to your data, always keep backup media in a secure area. A fireproof safe is perfect for storing important documents, but keep it separate from your computer.

Don't download or use pirated goods, including movies, music, and software, according to simple guidelines. You have no way of knowing if the material is malware-free, and in any event, much of it is illegal, as it frequently involves intellectual property theft. When pirated or criminal material is discovered on one of a company's computers, the legal responsibility falls on the company's owner, not the computer's user.

One of the most important goals of cyber security is to protect personally identifiable information (PII). Consider whether you should store the information on a device in the first place if it is particularly sensitive. If you answered yes, you should consider encrypting it. Always be cautious about what information you disclose and who you share it with. Consider where the information will be held and where it will end up if the person or organisation to whom you are entrusting it isn't as security conscious as you are.

Another issue to think about is file sharing. Cloud-based services are widely used to exchange information with friends, family, and co-workers. This is fine as long as you share material for genuine purposes and do not infringe on someone else's copyright. However, file sharing technologies are frequently used to illegally share material. Company employees who use personal cloud-based file sharing services from work have the additional risk of corporate data/information being stolen. Individual sharers host or seed films, audio recordings, books, and other media. The information is obtained by the user downloading a torrent file from a file sharing provider and running it through file sharing download software. The software connects to each seed machine and downloads little bits of the file, connecting them all. If it is not someone else's copyright or unless you have their specific permission, only share information with family, friends, and co-workers. If you must use a file sharing service, encrypt the data, especially if it is sensitive in any way, and utilise Multi Factor Authentication for both yourself and the recipient.

In recent years, the use of social media has skyrocketed. The most popular social networking sites include Facebook, Twitter, Flickr, LinkedIn, and Instagram, to name a few. While the purpose of these is to exchange information with friends, family, and co-workers, there are substantial risks associated with their use. First, if you have not appropriately specified your access preferences, you may not know who is viewing them (which may be difficult to identify). Many companies now look at job applicants' social media sites before determining whether or not to ask them for an interview. Second, you don't always know what other people are saying about you — that awkward photo from a recent night out may have been shot in jest, but it could indicate something about your personality that you'd rather keep private. Third, you may not be aware of the consequences of something you've said about someone else. Always be cautious about what you share on social media networking sites. It could come back to haunt you later. Keep a close eye on who you accept as a 'friend.' Make sure your information sharing preferences are set to the highest degree possible.

Free USB sticks should be avoided. Attendees will almost certainly receive a free USB memory stick with the presentations, as well as promotional and marketing materials given by the organisers and sponsors. It's possible that the memory stick contains malware, therefore it's a good idea to run it through a virus scanner on a separate computer before continuing to use it. It's important to remember that there is no such thing as a free lunch. Loading malware onto a USB memory stick and leaving it where their victim is likely to find it is a common fraud practised by the hacking community. Once plugged into the target's computer, the virus will install itself without the user's awareness and then remove itself from the memory stick, leaving no trace (assuming the attacker has done his work successfully). The malware can then get down to business. Before plugging a 'free' USB memory stick into any other computer, always test it on a stand-alone computer. If you find a memory stick lying around, don't use it because it could be a trap.

Banking applications can be troublesome as well. Banks are increasingly attempting to get consumers to use their online banking programmes, which can be accessed via desktop computers, mobile phones, and tablets. This is due to the fact that it saves them money. Fortunately, the programmes and online interfaces they offer have been properly tested and look to be reliable. Always remember to keep your banking information safe. When you've completed your transactions, log out of the banking application. Clear the cookies, browser history, and temporary internet files if you're using a public computer. Keep an eye out for people who are shoulder surfing, as they may be able to see what you are typing on your computer screen.

It's critical to lock your device. Physical locks are OK as long as no one can access your device without removing it. When the device is left unattended, it should be protected by a password and a password-protected screensaver should kick in at a sufficient period. Further security can be offered by instructing the device to erase its data after a certain number of failed password tries, however this must take into account the necessity to back up all data.

The importance of encryption cannot be overstated. Encryption is a relatively simple way to restrict unauthorised access to data on a computer, CD/DVD, or USB memory stick. There are two ways to accomplish this. When one or two files are confidential, it is simple to encrypt the individual files and securely distribute the encryption key to those who should have access. When there are several files that need to be protected, or when access to the computer's operating system or apps poses a substantial risk, the entire disc can be encrypted. When the user turns on the computer, he or she must first enter a boot-level password before the computer will even start.

Another thing to think about is operating systems and apps. An operating system is a software programme that runs on a computer. New or replacement operating systems should always be purchased or obtained from a reliable vendor, such as Microsoft or Apple for their operating systems and a range of trusted Linux vendors. It's critical to keep these operating systems up to date once they've been installed, and most vendors will give a free online updating system to do so if the facility has been enabled. The same can be said for critical applications. Regular updates contain not only fixes for issues, but also new features from time to time. Larger organisations should always test an updated operating system or application in a sterile environment before releasing it to the general public to verify that it does not interfere with existing corporate services.

To reduce the risk of malware, antivirus software should be installed. Antivirus software, according to some security experts, will only detect about 5% of viruses, but it is prudent to have it installed because failure to do so could result in a successful attack. It is critical to install regular antivirus updates (most antivirus software does this automatically) and to scan the computer on a regular basis in case a virus was already present when the antivirus software was brought up to date. Ascertain that operating systems and critical applications are always up to date. If at all possible, enable automatic updates. Ensure that your antivirus threat databases are up to date. While this does not ensure complete security, a decent antivirus system will detect the most common malware. Install a trustworthy antivirus programme. Many of these are available for no cost. Windows Defender includes an antivirus feature. In addition to antivirus protection, most antivirus packages include functions like URL inspection and protection while surfing the internet. Enable automatic updating to ensure that you have the most up-to-date virus profiles. Allow the software to scan the machine on a regular basis, ensuring that any malware that was there before a new virus was discovered is eliminated.

User Account Control (UAC) is an important factor to consider. Users with non-administrative access are unable to install software because of UAC. If several users share a computer, ensure sure all of their user accounts are non-administrative, and keep only one master administrative account that is used only when necessary. Even if you are the only user of a computer, you must create a non-administrative account and use it instead of the master administrative account, because unauthorised access to this account allows the user to assume entire control of the machine. Non-administrator users are automatically unable to install software on Apple computers, and the system can also be programmed to block an administrative user from installing software that does not originate from the Mac App Store or from an accredited developer.

Another control approach is the use of firewalls. If your computer has a built-in firewall, make sure it's turned on because it's typically extremely dependable. Defender is a built-in firewall that comes with Windows. There is no need to purchase third-party firewall software or enable the firewall that comes standard with many antivirus packages, as doing so may cause compatibility issues. The firewall can be set up to block or allow access to specific apps (through an administrative user account), adding an extra degree of security.

It's critical to keep your application software up to date. Reputable software providers will constantly give updates, not only when new features are added, but also when flaws in the software are discovered and resolved. If a well-known application, such as Microsoft Office or Adobe Acrobat, alerts you that an update is available, you should always accept it. Even better, if the operating system allows for automatic updates, this is worth enabling because it ensures that your applications are always up to date without you having to make a decision.

Many of the cyber security concerns we encounter are caused by user-related activities, such as the misuse – and even abuse – of networks, systems, and services. A considerable measure of self-discipline is required. Management is also responsible for keeping users on the straight and narrow, which entails monitoring user behaviour and, on occasion, taking corrective (perhaps disciplinary) action to remedy issues. Individual and corporate users can and should adhere to a variety of general rules.

Passwords, like toothbrushes, should be changed on a regular basis and should never be shared. Most people, including myself, have trouble remembering passwords. You must choose a username and password whenever you use a new online service, shop for goods, or register for information. This makes a lot of sense: it aids the supplier in identifying individual users; it keeps your transactions separate from those of others (at least in theory); and it gives you confidence as a user that the website you're using is relatively secure. Unfortunately, this means we have multiple usernames and passwords, and we have trouble remembering them all. As a result, we write them down somewhere, which is never a good idea because the piece of paper is likely to be found by someone who should not know your passwords, or it will be lost forever in the trash. The temptation is to use the same username and password for as many logins as possible, but this is the first step down a steep slope, since an attacker will have the opportunity to use it elsewhere if he finds one instance of it. Because many websites allow you to use your email address as your login, an attacker will often be able to guess it. If you do find yourself in the unfortunate position of having numerous passwords, there are a variety of solutions to make your life easier while maintaining a level of protection. All passwords that incorporate all or part of your name, family members' names (especially your mother's maiden name), and pets should be avoided. These are usually very simple to guess or find. If you must use basic passwords, choose ones that are difficult to guess, such as invented phrases like 'gunzleswiped,' and use a mix of upper and lower case letters, numerals, and other symbols whenever feasible. Passwords that are longer are always more secure than those that are shorter. Passwords should not be written down anywhere where they can be discovered by others. Use a password management tool if you find complicated passwords difficult to remember or if you have a big number of them. That way, you'll only need to remember one password to gain access. There are a plethora of such tools on the market.

When you're away from your computer and in a place where others might have access to it, screen locking is essential. Always use the screensaver, which is password-protected. This should be programmed to happen automatically after a predetermined amount of time on corporate user computers. Set a screensaver to cut in after no more than five minutes of idleness and safeguard it with a password. Configure a shortcut to start the screensaver if possible - a single keystroke or mouse movement will suffice. Never leave a computer unattended in a public place unless it has a password-protected screensaver and is physically locked.

When configuring new users on a system, the principle of least privilege must be observed. This means they only have the level of access they need, rather than being elevated to system administrator. When consumers acquire a new computer, it's all too common for them to set their personal account as the system administrator. Instead, they should use administrator credentials to set up the machine and then create their own user account without them. If someone else obtains that account's username and password, they will only be allowed to access a limited selection of system functions and will not be able to make system changes. Organizations with systems administrators must have two accounts, one with administrative access and one for day-to-day email and office work, as discussed earlier in the book. It should be a security policy norm that no one should ever use an account with elevated or administrator access for day-to-day tasks. Never give administrative access to a guest user on a computer. Password protection should always be enabled for guest user accounts. Always give a non-administrative account to the computer's main user. Only make necessary system modifications with the administration account user.

Online, cyber hygiene is critical. It's difficult to do anything these days without downloading images or documents due to the abundance of information available on the internet. Users should exercise caution when visiting and downloading from websites to ensure that they are visiting a legitimate site. There are proactive preventative steps that a user or organisation can take by implementing controls to lower the possibility of a successful attack, as well as simple procedures that users can take to avoid hazards while surfing the web. Pop-up windows containing malware, as well as scripts connecting to malware-infected websites, can be blocked by Internet browsers. Browsers with the 'protected' mode enable anonymous web browsing. It isn't 100% effective, but it should keep your computer's identity hidden from inquisitive eyes.

To protect young web surfers, parental controls can be implemented in both Microsoft Windows and Apple operating systems. When we use the internet, we are subjected to intrusions such as adware and spyware. Much of this may be turned off in the browser, for example, by turning off pop-up windows.

It is critical to encrypt data that is stored and shared. Encryption scrambles information, usually referred to as 'plain text,' so that it cannot be read or changed by unauthorised parties. To encrypt data, a 'key' – generally a large number – is used in conjunction with software called an encryption algorithm to convert plain text to encrypted text. Only the correct key in combination with the same algorithm can decrypt the cypher text. To ensure confidentiality, two different types of encryption are utilised. Symmetric encryption is when the sender and receiver of data share the same key. Because more than one person has access to symmetric encryption keys, they are more likely to be detected. As a result, they must be replaced at regular intervals, such as daily, or even each time they are used. Asymmetric encryption, often known as public key encryption, is a type of encryption in which both the sender and the recipient have two keys, one of which is made public and the other kept secret. The sender encrypts the information with the receiver's public key, and the recipient decrypts it with the recipient's private key. A one-way encryption approach is employed to maintain integrity, in which a key is utilised in conjunction with a so-called hashing algorithm that scrambles plain text in such a way that it cannot be reversed. Hard disc drive encryption, in which the entire hard disc drive or chosen files are encrypted, is an example of this sort of encryption. BitLocker is used by Microsoft Windows, while FileVault is incorporated into Apple's operating system. The user enters their password, which is subsequently hashed, and the resulting hash value is compared to a previously stored value. Because information is typically stored in locations over which users have no control, storing it on the cloud necessitates that it be secured.

Another consideration is remote work. It's always tempting to use 'free' Wi-Fi at coffee shops or hotels whenever we have the chance, but this comes with its own set of risks, such as an attacker intercepting data being transmitted between the device and the access point, attempting to recover the encryption key in use (if one exists), and using the recovered key to gain access to the user's information. Do not use free Wi-Fi for any financial transactions that require the transmission of your bank or credit card information. Any service that does not have an encryption key should be avoided. Most bars and restaurants that offer free Wi-Fi, for example, will always use an encryption key to prevent 'drive-by' users from accessing the network. If a Wi-Fi hotspot is required for corporate network users, a virtual private network (VPN) back to the corporate network should always be employed. Furthermore, corporate PCs should always be set to prevent split tunnelling, so that when a VPN is in operation, all traffic is routed through the VPN. In terms of Wi-Fi in the home and at work, most home broadband services nowadays provide users with a router that includes a wireless access point as well as Ethernet ports, which is a much more convenient method of connecting in many ways because we can move around the house without having to connect to the internet in each room. When setting up wireless networks in the home and workplace, there are a few basic principles to follow. Begin by altering the router's SSID name. Avoid using a name that could be used to identify your property. Change the administration username (if possible) and definitely the password after setting up the router or wireless access points. Recommendations can be found in the prior debate about user passwords. Use a long and difficult key to prevent people from using your wireless network without permission, as you never know what they'll do. The default key will most likely be printed on the side of the router by the router's manufacturer, and you'll need to use it to set it up, but it's critical to change it afterwards. Turn off remote administration if your router has it. You can turn it on locally until you've finished what you need to do if you ever require it. Turn off Universal Plug 'n' Play if your router supports it, as it is a completely unsecure protocol. If you don't need to use Wi-Fi Protected Setup (WPS) to connect to a wireless printer, you should switch it off because it adds another layer of security.

Bluetooth is well-known for its flaws. Individuals have minimal control over the security of their Bluetooth gadgets. In some cases, the only options for the user are 'on' or 'off.' A few tips should help to lessen the possibility of Bluetooth issues. Make sure the Bluetooth device (such as a smartphone) is password-protected. Reject all connection requests from devices you are unfamiliar with. If you misplace a Bluetooth device (such as a headset), remove it from your list of linked devices so that it can't connect to yours. When you're not utilising Bluetooth-enabled devices, turn them off.

Mobile devices use GPS to determine their location, such as when using a mapping application to design a path between two points. This is called location services. When you install many smartphone and tablet apps, they turn on location services by default, allowing them to follow your movements. This may be necessary in some cases, such as the one described above, but there is no reason why a smartphone game should require it. Consider each app on your smartphone or tablet carefully, and decide whether location services will improve your experience or merely give out information about where you are. Turn off location services in the general settings menu for any apps that you don't think should be using them. If the application requires it, it will prompt you to enable them, and you can choose whether or not to do so.

Information Security Management – Large Organisations

To maintain excellent cyber defences, larger organisations will need to engage in more major actions. First and first, businesses must comprehend their data. It's critical for businesses to understand the nature of the data they have under their control. This will include not just their own information, but also information for which they are regarded data processors under data protection regulation, or information that they are simply holding, as in the case of a cloud provider. Second, businesses must safeguard their data rather than merely the perimeter. Many companies focus on preventing unauthorised access from outside the network without realising that insiders might be just as hazardous. While it is critical to defend the organization's network perimeter, it is also critical to guarantee that internal access to information is protected, primarily through the use of carefully enforced access rights.

Organizations should create and maintain security policies, which will set the tone for any future rules that may be required. Security policies, in general, do not need to be long papers because they do not require a lot of detail – this may be included in lower-level documents like processes, procedures, and work instructions. A security policy should generally include an overview, its purpose, its scope (what is included and what is excluded), the policy statements themselves (which form the main body), requirements for compliance (including penalties for non-compliance), any related policies, definitions of terms used, and revision history for ease of use and clarity. In most policy statements, it is stated that the organization's information must be protected in accordance with all applicable legislation, sector rules, company policies, and international standards, particularly those relating to data protection, human rights, and information freedom. Typically, policy statements specify that each of the organization's information assets will be assigned to a designated information owner who will be responsible for establishing the asset's appropriate uses and ensuring that adequate security measures are in place to secure it. Only those with a legitimate business need will have access to the organization's information. All of the organization's data will be classified according to a level of privacy and sensitivity that is acceptable. At all times, the integrity of the organization's information assets must be maintained. Individuals who have been given access to information are responsible for handling it properly and according to the classification. Unauthorized access to the organization's information must be prevented. The organization's information security policies will be strictly enforced.

Directive policies (say 'thou must' or 'thou shalt not'), administrative policies (underpinned by an admin function), communal policies (where vast elements of the organisation work together), and technical policies are the four types of organisational security measures (require specific hardware, software or both).

The following rules and controls are common in SMEs and large organisations: Individual behaviours are the focus of directive policies, which tell people what they should or should not do. As with any policies, there should be some mention of the repercussions of not adhering to them, as well as the consequences of not adhering to them.

Acceptable usage standards apply to all users of the organization's network and services, whether they are temporary employees, contractors, or permanent employees. Personal internet access (browsing, shopping, etc.) and email are typically considered acceptable uses. It could also include the utilisation of organisational resources while posting to blogs and social media sites.

The duration for which information can be held and how it should be disposed of when the retention period expires are determined by the information retention policy. This policy shall be tightly linked to the Information Classification Policy and any applicable data protection legislation. The organization's data and information retention policy will be closely linked to its Information Classification Policy, and it will need to take into account the requirements of data protection, human rights, and freedom of information legislation where applicable, as this will affect the amount of time personal information can be kept.

This is followed up with information classification policy. The organisation is likely to have a variety of sorts of data, including publicly available data, data that should be restricted to all employees, and data that should be provided only to a small number of employees. These categories should be defined in the information classification policy, rather than using generic phrases like confidential or restricted which might have various meanings not only between the public and private sectors, but also within similar organisations. The policy will specify how and where information is stored (and, in certain situations, not stored); its retention term; how it is tagged; the extent to which it may be shared; how and where it must be backed up; how it is transmitted; and, lastly, how it is destroyed when no longer required.

Administrative policies are primarily concerned with the actions that people or groups of persons take to defend the organisation as a whole. Instead of determining the dos and don'ts of individual users, these policies will govern the capabilities of all users inside the organisation.

Access control governs how programmes and data are accessible, and it can be done in a variety of ways, including role-based, time of day or date, level of privilege, and whether access is read-only or read-write. Different means of authentication, such as single sign-on, digital certificates, biometrics, and token-based authentication, can all be included in an access control policy.

Controlling change is critical. Changes that are uncontrolled are a common source of difficulties in systems and services. The method for making changes to the systems and their supporting network, including the operating system and applications, will be described in the change control policy. This may entail a thorough examination of the proposals prior to any attempt at implementation, as well as functional and load testing prior to implementation. Change management goes hand in hand with change control, and it entails notifying users of upcoming changes and having a back-out process in place should the change fail for any reason.

When employees depart the company, access termination must take place. Existing permissions should be cancelled (rather than updated) when an employee changes to a new department or a new role within an existing department. Permissions should then be reinstated at levels relevant to the new role.

Viruses and malware can attack systems without warning and require a structured strategy rather than an ad hoc one that could cause more harm than benefit. The policy will specify who will deal with the situation and the steps they will take to identify the virus, isolate it if possible, and eliminate or quarantine it.

Password management is an important component of information security policy that is often disregarded. Password management is famously problematic among users. They'll use passwords that are easy to remember, such as their mother's maiden name, their birthdate, or the name of their pet (if they can get away with it), all of which are pretty easy for an attacker to guess or uncover. Users should be informed about the risks of this activity and given instructions on how to construct secure passwords. The standard recommendation in the past has always been to establish a minimum password length, to employ a complicated combination of letters, numbers, and other symbols, and to force the user to change their password at regular intervals.

The burden of proof should be placed on the verifier. It is far easier to design a single piece of software than it is to require hundreds or thousands of people to follow a set of rules, and the users will be less stressed as a result. The length of a password is critical. Check the length of users' passwords and encourage them to choose longer ones. Users' passwords are checked against a dictionary list of known poor or bad passwords, and if the test is affirmative, the users are required to try again. Wherever practical, use Multi Factor Authentication on your platforms.

Overly complex password composition guidelines should be avoided by businesses. These make it impossible for users to remember passwords (especially if distinct passwords are required for each application) and may force them to write them down. Where password management technologies have been proved to be effective, they can be allowed. Password hints can help users remember their passwords, but they can also provide an attacker information about their passwords. Because the perpetrator of a targeted assault is likely to have done extensive research on their intended victim, such evidence could quickly reveal the user's credentials. Credentials chosen from a list have a similar questionable value. A serious assailant is just as likely to know your mother's maiden name, town of birth, first school name, and so on as the indicators listed above. Password expiration after a certain amount of time offers little to increase password security and just adds to the user's confusion. Users should be able to change their password if they believe it has been compromised, but forcing them to do so without justification adds to their burden.

A statement about changing default passwords, particularly those that grant root access to computers and network devices like firewalls and routers, should be included in the policy. Passwords are sometimes integrated within apps, especially when one application has to connect to another and exchange data without human interaction. Embedded passwords should be avoided wherever feasible because they are likely to be generally known and hence offer a potential attack vector; nonetheless, if they must be used, they should be altered from the manufacturer's default. A 'brute force' search, in which an attacker's computer tries every possible combination of characters until it finds the appropriate one, can break any password. Long passwords will make this much more difficult, and the attacker may simply give up and move on to a less difficult victim. Users also have a tendency to reuse passwords across numerous systems. Attackers are aware of this, and if they learn one of a user's passwords, they can usually gain access to other systems as well. Each system to which a user need access should have its own password. A password management tool may be an effective solution if users must have several passwords and have trouble remembering them all. Single sign-on, on the other hand, is a way for dealing with numerous password difficulties.

Reusing passwords should also be discouraged, and some access control systems, such as Microsoft's Active Directory, can be configured to restrict reuse after a particular amount of time. As previously reported, NIST is working on new password rules, which, while not yet formally published at the time of writing, are worth looking into.

External disc drives, USB memory sticks and other removable storage can be a source of malware if infected on another device outside the organisation, as well as a way for users to remove information from the organisation without permission. Many USB gadgets, including smartphones, tablet computers, and even e-cigarettes, can readily act as removable media and become a source of malware, despite not being clearly labelled as such. Unless the user has a very particular, authorised requirement, system hardware can readily be modified to block the usage of removable media.

Staff can transport huge files around the organisation using shared network drives. They do, however, have one major flaw: there is frequently no audit trail of who transferred information onto the hard disc and then copied them off. Furthermore, worms and other types of malware can infect numerous shared discs inside a network. If files are to be shared between internal and external users, a collaborative system such as Microsoft SharePoint should be considered, as it allows the organisation to choose who can use the system to exchange files and keep track of who did what and when.

Segregating duties is crucial. It's common for companies to assign IT experts to a variety of positions, which can be a mistake in some cases because it gives administration-level users the ability to establish and assign high-level user accounts to people who don't need them or shouldn't have them. This gives a member of staff the ability to both order and authorise the purchase of products, which can lead to fraud. The best way to deal with this is to make sure that a single user account can't do both jobs - in other words, to entirely separate the responsibilities and access permissions of two different account types.

Backup and restore are significant considerations. Backup intervals (which may differ for different information elements); backup method (for example, full or incremental); backup media; whether backup media is kept on the organization's premises (but not the same location as the data being backed up) or at a third-party location; the maximum time allowed for recovering the data. Most major organisations will have a backup policy in place, but like all policies, it should be evaluated on a regular basis to ensure that the correct systems are being backed up to removable (encrypted) media and kept off-site in a safe location. However, many organisations have realised to their cost that some backup tapes or discs cannot be read after a period of time, making it necessary to undertake a test restoral of data at regular intervals as a sanity check. While using cloud services to retain a long-term repository of data may be a cost-effective solution, it does necessitate careful planning and administration, because it is frequently quite easy to delete information saved in the cloud, which negates the purpose of the exercise. Another increasingly popular option is when the move to virtualization has occurred and storage area networks (SANs) are becoming more widely employed, with a backup SAN. The SAN can be updated on a daily basis or at frequent intervals during the day. Additional backups to different media, on the other hand, are usually suggested.

Another element is antivirus software. Some businesses have begun to abandon antivirus software after hearing reports in the media about its ineffectiveness, particularly when new malware emerges that the antivirus software author has failed to address. These are characterised as 'zero-day' vulnerabilities since the creator has no time to repair them once they are discovered.

Even if antivirus software does not find and catch every vulnerability, it will prevent known vulnerabilities from generating problems by neutralising or quarantining the offending virus, therefore it is still important having an antivirus capability and making sure it is kept up to date.

Updates to software are critical. Many important applications are all targets for attackers looking for flaws. Organizations must keep these operating systems and applications up to date with the most recent patches. If this isn't done, an attacker may be able to exploit the time between when the vulnerability is discovered and when the patch is applied to correct it. Automatic updating should be used wherever possible and practical, as it eliminates the need for additional human input from support employees and lowers the 'patch gap.' Furthermore, any software upgrade that may result in a significant change to the operating system or apps should have a back-out plan in place so that the organisation can easily restore to the previous version.

It is necessary to arrange for remote access. Whether or whether a company uses VPNs for network access, it must establish how employees and third-party contractors can access information, as well as the network and its processes. Other rules, such as access control, security awareness, and passwords, will be tightly linked to this policy.

Wireless and mobile gadgets must be regulated as well. The policy must specify the organization's requirements for installing wireless access points throughout its facilities, as well as how the wireless infrastructure devices must be configured and secured, including the encryption method, whether the SSID should be broadcast, and which bands and channels should be used. When it comes to devices that use Bluetooth for communication, it should only be enabled when absolutely necessary and then shut off. The organisation should set the device's visibility to 'Hidden' once it is configured for use so that it cannot be scanned by other Bluetooth devices. If device pairing is required, all devices must be set to 'Unauthorized,' which means that each connection request must be authorised. Unsigned applications and those received from unknown sources should be denied. There will need to be a portion in the policy for mobile devices given by the organisation that limits when and when they can be used over wireless networks that are not owned or provided by the organisation, such as public wireless or third-party networks. This policy will also define what information can be saved on the device, what programmes can be placed onto it, if it can be used to access the internet, and whether the data stored on the device is or will become the organization's intellectual property.

The bring your own device (BYOD) policy may overlap slightly here, but in this situation, the device – such as a laptop computer, tablet computer, or smartphone – will be the employee's personal property rather than the company's. The policy may include provisions for use by friends or family members, as well as distinct login processes for access to the organization's network and, if necessary, hard disc drive encryption.

It is necessary to police our peripherals. Many operating systems have auxiliary services that aren't necessary for the system's operation but present attack vectors. System administrators can disable and remove unwanted services and peripherals from users' computers, such as USB ports, SD card slots, and CD/DVD drives, which cannot be enabled or utilised once they are removed. This policy could be part of a larger IT infrastructure procurement policy for the company.

It is critical to isolate compromised systems. Organizations that discover a compromised machine must isolate it from the rest of the network as soon as feasible to prevent malware from propagating to other computers on the network. After the malware has been eradicated, a forensic investigation of the system should be performed, preferably by a professional organisation if the necessary capabilities are not available internally, and the systems should then be restored to normal operation using trusted media.

Add-ons and extensions for the browser must be taken into account. Attacks on internet browsers, add-ons, and extensions are growing more common, and it's vital that attackers can't obtain access to systems by exploiting flaws in software like Microsoft's Internet Explorer, Adobe's Acrobat Reader, or Adobe Flash. Patches should be installed as soon as they become available using the vendor's automatic update or software distribution mechanisms.

AutoRun is a feature of Microsoft Windows that allows a command file on a USB memory stick, CD, or DVD to be executed automatically when it is inserted into the computer. Because the user may be completely unconscious that the media is infected and unaware that the software is running, this is a very simple technique for an attacker to acquire access to a system. AutoRun deactivation will most likely be a minor annoyance for both users and system administrators.

Another attack vector is Adobe Acrobat Reader. Adobe's Portable Document Format (PDF) has established itself as the de facto standard for information sharing. Almost any file, presentation, or document can be exported or converted to PDF format, which looks the same on any computer, smartphone, or tablet with Acrobat Reader installed. However, a growing number of cyber-attacks are being carried out by embedding malware in PDF documents and then transferring them to the device. Organizations can harden Acrobat Reader to safeguard their machines from assaults contained inside PDF files.

Outsourcing has the potential to compromise security. Certain areas of an organization's operations may be more cost-effective to outsource. This is becoming more common in the case of an organization's ICT infrastructure and outsource service providers may offer to provide not only data storage, but also operating system hardware and software, as well as application software. This may be offered at a specific third-party site, as is common in disaster recovery plans, or in a more virtual setting, such as cloud services. In either case, it will be critical that the organisation has a clear policy regarding the selection of suppliers for this type of service, which will form the basis of a service level agreement (SLA) and should also include an exit policy should the organisation decide to move away from a supplier, particularly with regard to ownership of indexing to the organization's information and subsequent destruction of any information remaining in the cloud.

Communal policies are those that have the potential to affect not only individuals within an organisation, but also the business's larger context and the environment in which it operates.

During the specified hours of operation, contingency planning establishes how data or system access is made available to users. The policy will outline the steps that must be taken to guarantee that access is maintained in the event that the systems or the methods of accessing them, such as a web server and its supporting network, fail. A business continuity or catastrophe recovery policy will almost always be linked to a contingency planning policy.

A policy for incident response will outline how occurrences are reported, investigated, and addressed. Additional steps, such as business continuity and disaster recovery plans, may be required if certain pre-set failure thresholds are surpassed. An incident may also necessitate the dissemination of information about the incident to employees, customers, third-party suppliers, the general public, and, if the organisation is in a highly regulated sector (such as energy, finance, or transportation), the incident may necessitate notification to the sector regulator. Incident response plans, like business continuity and disaster recovery plans, should be reviewed and tested on a regular basis or whenever a major component of the organization's operation changes.

Staff behaviour is greatly influenced by security education, awareness, and training. Because many of the cyber security challenges we encounter are created by users, educating them on the dangers they face, including threats, vulnerabilities, and potential consequences, is a critical first step toward improving cyber security. The first phase is awareness, which gradually introduces users to the information and concepts they need to know so that security becomes second nature to them, and they stop cultivating harmful security habits and move toward a position where they are totally dedicated to good security practise. This is then augmented with training for individuals who are more directly involved in day-to-day security operations and require specialised training to adequately fulfil their roles.

Technical policies are those that are strictly technical. They may be required in order for other policies previously stated to function properly, or they may be sufficient on their own.

Spam email filtering is essential because spam is inconvenient. It might range from somewhat irritating to downright frightening. Most email service providers now scan emails as they flow through their systems, removing any that have been previously reported as spam. This, however, may not eliminate all spam email, as fresh spam messages will always appear, and some filters may never add them to their blacklist, or the spam may take time to be reported. It is critical to teach people how to recognise spam and junk mail as part of the organization's awareness programme, even if it comes from a recognised and generally trusted source.

In the event of a security problem, audit trails allow an organisation to follow a chain of events and, if necessary, show that a person performed or did not do a certain action. In circumstances where legal actions are involved, such evidence may be necessary, in which case the audit trail must also be forensically sound.

Firewall policies will dictate how firewalls are deployed and configured to become an integrated part of the network, particularly in terms of the rules that must be enforced and maintained. All inbound connections from the internet to services that the organisation does not want to be available should be blocked using firewalls. All incoming connections should be blocked by default, and only those services that the organisation explicitly chooses to give to the outside world should be authorised. In addition, the IP address of the incoming session should be a genuine public IP address rather than an IP address linked with the company. If the company has a block of 32 public IP addresses, for example, these must be filtered out. In addition to firewalls, it may be beneficial to divide the organization's network into distinct sections by function, such as research and development, operations, and finance, making it more difficult for an attacker to access a specific service (see the later item on VPNs). It's also typical for businesses to use a so-called demilitarised zone, or DMZ, to build another barrier between their exterior and internal networks. Any outbound connection from the organisation to the internet should also start from a specialised proxy server or service located in a DMZ rather than on the main network. Firewalls are available in a variety of shapes and sizes. Many of them require specialised hardware to run on, as well as well-trained personnel to configure and maintain them. Because it must not only defend the organisation from unwanted incursion, but also meet the business demands in terms of what can and cannot be sent through it, the decision on which sort of firewall to use and how it should be set is best left to expert counsel. Other firewalls are included with desktop operating systems, making them easier to use and requiring little to no setting. These should always be enabled on user PCs, and the user's access should prohibit them from altering it by giving them a non-administrative account.

Encryption is a valuable weapon in our arsenal. An information encryption policy will work hand in hand with an information classification policy in that it will specify how sensitive information will be encrypted and how encryption keys will be managed and exchanged for specific levels of information classification (for example, secret or top secret). For example, information classified at a certain level could be exchanged between two people using a simple encryption mechanism like PGP, with each person owning their own encryption keys, whereas other information might necessitate the use of a public key management system, with encryption keys managed and distributed centrally. In addition, the policy should distinguish between information in transit (for example, within emails) and information at rest, which is saved on hard drives or other media, particularly if it is stored in the cloud. Encrypting the hard disc of a mobile user's computer for information at rest is reasonably simple, and it implies that the device cannot be used without the user's password to decrypt the data, rendering the data useless to anyone who takes it. FileVault is a feature on Apple computers that encrypts the entire hard drive. BitLocker is a security feature available to Windows users. Because it is never certain which country or countries the cloud storage is hosted in, and those countries' jurisdictions may not provide a sufficient level of protection on data, even to the point of intercepting and analysing it themselves, business data stored in the cloud should always be encrypted. Sensitive data that is sent to another place – whether through memory stick or email – should always be encrypted, so that anyone who can intercept the transmission or steal the media is unable to access the data. The keys used in symmetric encryption algorithms like Data Encryption Standard (DES), 3DES, and AES are typically 56, 112, 128 or 256 bits long, whereas the keys used in asymmetric or public key cryptography (typically 2048 bits long) are used in the initial setup of an encrypted session to determine the actual fixed encryption key that will be used by the symmetric algorithm during the session. These keys aren't usually utilised for main encryption because they take up too much processing power.

SSH (Secure Socket Shell) is a network protocol that allows administrators to access remote systems in a secure manner. It allows two systems to communicate via an insecure network, like as the internet, with robust authentication and encrypted communication. It is frequently used by network administrators for remote system and application management, allowing them to log on to another machine, run commands, and transfer files across systems.

Between two communication programmes sharing information, such as a user's web browser and an online banking or e-commerce application, the Transport Layer Security (TLS) protocol ensures both secrecy and integrity. VPN connections, instant messaging services, and Voice-Over-IP (VoIP) applications all employ TLS. To protect the transmissions, both SSH and TLS require encryption keys (as stated above), which are typically 256 bits in length. It's not uncommon for SSH and TLS keys to be misused. It is advised that organisations rotate SSH and TLS keys at intervals to limit the likelihood of insiders exploiting these after they leave the company, exposing crucial network infrastructure to unwanted access.

Digital certificates are commonly used to verify websites, especially when conducting financial transactions. Both individuals and businesses can obtain digital certificates from recognised certification authority (CAs). However, it is critical to remember to renew the certificate on a regular basis (usually once a year), as failure to do so renders the certificate unusable, and users whose web browser detects this will receive an alert that the certificate has expired. As a result, they may decide not to complete the online transaction.

Another attack vector is email attachments. Employees should be taught not to open email attachments unless they are expecting them during awareness training. Furthermore, users should not be allowed to run software downloaded from the internet unless it has been scanned for viruses and tested for security flaws. Visitors to a hacked website may unwittingly introduce malware. Email servers should be configured to prevent or discard emails with file attachments that are widely used to propagate malware, such as.vbs,.bat,.exe,.pif,.zip, and .scr files.

Network security policies cover a wide range of topics, including how firewalls, intrusion detection software, antivirus software, operating system and application patching, and password protection can be used to safeguard an organization's networks from infiltration. Fixed and wireless local area networks (LANs), VPNs, wide area networks (WANs), and storage area networks (SANs) should all be included.

Virtual private networks (VPNs) are widely used, and a policy will be necessary that specifies how and where they are implemented, as well as who may use them (for example, for remote access by employees, guests, and third-party contractors) and how they are configured and secured. VPNs should be used as part of a plan that also includes network segregation and firewall deployment.

Physical security guards, perimeter fencing and gates with movement detection and/ or CCTV systems and electronically controlled gates are all examples of physical access control. Electronic door access systems, whether via personal identification number (PIN), wireless proximity card, or a combination of both, will often govern physical access control within the organization's sites. Individual members of employees, guests, and contractors will have different levels and locations of access depending on the supporting system. Internally, infrared movement detection and CCTV systems are frequently used, particularly in high-risk areas.

Intrusion detection systems (IDS) assist by attempting to detect unauthorised intrusion into a network or computer system. IDS come in a variety of shapes and sizes. Individual computer systems have host intrusion detection systems (HIDS) installed on them that only monitor the configuration of that system. When a HIDS detects an unusual change in a system's configuration, it sends an alarm message to a console, which a security operator can investigate. In order to identify aberrant network activity, such as attacks on firewalls, network intrusion detection systems (NIDS) are placed on internal networks and subnetworks. If they detect an attack, they will also report it to a console, but they will also be able to take action, such as changing firewall rules. Under specific circumstances, forensic techniques may be required, as well as the retention of hard drives and data for possible use in legal actions.

Information Management

Security, in order to be improved, must be cautious about information sharing. This paradox can lead to disputes in the cyber security industry, as well as the withholding of knowledge about certain vulnerabilities on occasion. Let's start with the most fundamental features of information exchange. The exchange of information is dependent on trust. This can be on a personal basis, with one person trusting another, or between groups of people inside organisations who have a shared interest in the issue. Information that is to be given must be classified in some way. Many information sharing projects now employ the so-called "Traffic Light Protocol" (TLP) to identify how information must be treated before being shared. It's crucial that the data is correct. It is futile to share unverified information because it wastes time and resources. Other people's advice must be given at the appropriate moment. It's pointless to conceal knowledge from individuals who could benefit from it, because an attacker could become aware of it and exploit the time lag to launch a successful attack. It is necessary to share with caution. The circle of interested parties with whom the information is shared must be trusted to handle it in a mutually agreed-upon manner and to keep it out of the wrong hands. Mechanisms should be put into the process to prohibit dissemination to people or organisations who are not part of the sharing group. It should be able to conceal the information's source. In some cases, disclosing the identity of the organisation that highlighted the issue could be harmful, hence a method of disseminating information without credit is necessary. Information should be able to be shared with other essential infrastructure sectors. There are frequently issues in cyber security that will affect many, if not all, critical infrastructure sectors, and a way to exchange information between them in a controlled manner is vital.

An information sharing community's members must have complete trust in one another. But what exactly does trust mean? The firm belief in someone or something's reliability, veracity, or capacity is known as trust. In the context of cyber security, this means that we must trust not only the information we get, but also the source of that information, whether an individual or an organisation. When information is shared face-to-face, the so-called 'Chatham House Rule' is frequently followed. When a meeting, or a portion of one, is held under the Chatham House Rule, participants are allowed to use the information they hear, but neither the speaker(s) nor any other participant's identity or affiliation may be divulged. At meetings, the world-famous Chatham House Rule can be invoked to foster transparency and information sharing. When it comes to the classification of information to be given, there are two levels of trust. To begin, the originator must ensure that the information has been accurately classified and that the recipients will treat the data in accordance with that classification. Second, recipients must have sufficient faith in the originator's integrity in order to have the same level of confidence in the information's correctness and reliability. The capacity to have an independent party, trusted by all members of an information sharing community, who can operate as a moderator and also act as a go-between in specific situations, as we will see later, is the final feature of trust. The Trust Master is another name for this person.

The classification of information is critical. Information to be shared must be classified according to its sensitivity, and whichever method is used, it must be able to be used by both the public and private sectors without requiring them to cross-reference respective classification schemes. The Traffic Light Protocol is a simple example that is utilised by many information sharing projects that categorises data into four different colours. The colour red denotes that it is intended solely for specific recipients. In the case of a face-to-face meeting, for example, dissemination of red-coded information is limited to those in attendance, and in most cases, information will be conveyed verbally or in person. Amber denotes restricted dissemination, with recipients having permission to share amber information with others inside their organisation only if they have a 'need-to-know' basis. The originator may be requested to identify the sharing's intended boundaries. The colour green denotes community-wide, implying that knowledge in this category can be broadly disseminated within a community or organisation. The information, however, may not be published or placed on the internet, nor may it be distributed outside of the community. Finally, the white colour denotes unrestricted sharing. Subject to ordinary copyright regulations, white information may be freely distributed. This information classification approach is very fundamental and extensively used in information sharing since it is easy to understand and implement, and it can also be used to other industries or countries. The creator of the material to be shared will usually choose the classification colour, however Trust Masters may choose to raise it if they believe it is set too low.

Information protection is an important factor to consider. When sharing information, the creator may believe it is vital to limit its further dissemination or to ensure that the information can be revoked or destroyed if it is no longer valid or if the level of sensitivity has changed. This can be accomplished through the use of a mechanism known as 'information rights management,' which encrypts material – such as a text document – and allows receivers to open it as long as they can identify themselves to the central sharing resource. Additionally, the document can be protected such that it can never be copied, including the copying of chosen parts of the document and therefore preventing it from being inserted into an unprotected document; or printed, prohibiting its physical or scanned distribution. If the document is forwarded to another recipient, they will need access rights to the central sharing resource, and if the originator decides to delete the original document, any remaining copies will be unable to be opened because the original document's decryption metadata will be deleted as well. Similarly, to information categorization, originators must ensure that information is suitably safeguarded, and recipients must have sufficient faith in the integrity of the originator to have the same level of confidence in the information's correctness and reliability. Running all incoming or outgoing emails through a scanning system that can detect and isolate any message containing specific words or phrases, or that can direct encrypted messages to a central verification point prior to release, makes good business sense in organisations that have a strict requirement for confidentiality.

Anonymization is a critical component of data security. There can be times when businesses do not want to be associated with an attack or another cyber security incident in which they have become involved. The reasons for this include business interests, and companies may be hesitant to let competitors know who was affected by the occurrence since it could put them at a competitive disadvantage or harm their stock price or public reputation. However, they may still want information about the exploit to be made available to the general public. In a face-to-face situation, such a company can approach the Trust Master and request that they report the issue without naming the source. The Trust Master will go to considerable lengths to guarantee that the originator's request for anonymity is honoured, ensuring that the information sent on contains no clues or additional metadata that might reveal, infer, suggest, or identify the originator in any manner. In the case of a centralised information sharing system, the Trust Master's duty must be fulfilled by the system itself in collaboration with the information's originator. When setting up the specific information to be shared, the originator could choose the 'anonymize' option in the system's options. This will delete any traces of who supplied the data in the first place. If the material includes other documents, such as word-processed documents, spreadsheets, or presentations, the source is responsible for completely anonymizing these as well. Instead, the originator could choose the 'anonymize via the Trust Master' option. In this case, the originator delivers the information to the Trust Master in an open manner, and the Trust Master subsequently presents it to the community as though it came from the Trust Master alone. The creators must make sure that nothing in the information they're sharing can betray their identity, and that their identity can't be deduced from the content detail. They must also believe that their identity will not be revealed by the information sharing mechanism or the Trust Master. The recipient does not need to have any further trust in this situation. Some cyber security situational submissions will inevitably be of significant interest to other sectors and sharing information with them would be highly beneficial if not essential, and this can often avoid possible duplication of effort. Organizations, or groups of communities, who wish to provide their own centralised systems for information sharing may later wish to interconnect these so that they can broaden the scope of their operations. Contact and trust may already exist between these various groups, communities, or sectors, in which case information may be freely shared between them, subject to the same rules that govern sharing within a sector. Alternatively, if no prior contact has been established and hence no level of trust exists, the Trust Masters in those sectors seeking to share information can act as intermediaries and commence a limited amount of information sharing, gradually expanding bilateral information sharing as trust grows. Finally, once the sectors' trust has been established, the Trust Masters can create preferences in the information sharing system that allow individual sector users to share information with a peer in another sector on a one-to-one basis or with the entire sector. Information creators should have the same level of trust in consumers from other industries as they do for users from their own. In the same way, the data should be categorised, safeguarded, and anonymized. From the recipient's perspective, the only thing that matters is that they believe the information's originators, and thus the information itself.

Information about cyber security issues can be shared, and in the UK, this is frequently done through WARPS (warning, advice, and reporting points), CiSP (Cyber Security Information Sharing Partnership), CERTs (computer emergency response teams), and computer security incident response teams (CSIRTs), or security information exchanges (SIEs) or information sharing and analysis centres (ISACs).

WARPs are a UK effort that started under the National Infrastructure Security Coordination Centre's auspices (NISCC). Members of WARPs can get and share up-to-date cyber threat information and best practises. CiSP from CERT-UK now offers WARPs. Regional governments, emergency services, and military organisations make up the majority of current WARP members.

CiSP is a collaboration between the UK government and industry to share cyber security threat and vulnerability information. The goal is to raise situational awareness of cyber risks, lowering the impact on UK enterprises as a result. Only UK registered firms responsible for the management of an electronic communications network in the UK, or organisations sponsored by a government department, an existing CiSP member, or a trade body or association, are eligible for CiSP membership. Members of the CiSP can exchange cyber threat information in real time, in a secure environment, and under a framework that ensures confidentiality. Alerts and advisories, weekly and monthly summaries, and trend analysis reporting are all examples of information presented.

CERTs have been around for a long and were founded by Carnegie Mellon University in the United States. The practise of gathering, analysing, and disseminating security alerts has had a significant impact on all sectors around the world. The CSIRTs serve the same purpose, and the mnemonics are interchangeable. Many governments now have CERT/CSIRTs in place, and some bigger multinational corporations with operations that cross traditional national and continental borders may do so as well. In the United Kingdom, CERT-UK is responsible for national cyber security incident management, support to critical national infrastructure companies dealing with cyber security incidents, promoting cyber security situational awareness, and serving as the single international point of contact for coordination and collaboration between national CERTs, all of which are derived from the UK's Cyber Security Strategy.

Almost any individual or organisation interested in receiving updates can subscribe to a CERT or CSIRT. The amount and frequency of updates, on the other hand, might be overpowering at times. CERT-UK delivers alerts with guidance in the event of a catastrophic national cyber security incident, advisories that address detected cyber security issues, and best practise advise on a variety of cyber issues through CiSP.

SIEs and ISACs exist exclusively to facilitate the exchange of threat, vulnerability, and incident information. SIEs typically provide raw data on occurrences, but ISACs typically provide a more in-depth analysis and response recommendations. SIEs and ISACs typically include both public and private sector organisations that are part of key national infrastructure, as well as their main government agency and any other organisation with a legitimate interest in the sector's security including regulators.

Security Education, Awareness And Training

Our end users are one of the most common sources of cyber-attacks. They may not do it on purpose, but they frequently commit unintended acts of cyber vandalism that generate endless issues for IT and security support employees. They act incorrectly and release or enable information to be released as a result of their actions or inactions, however this is typically owing to the fact that they have not been properly trained by the organisation to respond appropriately to information security events. Some of this may be remedied by educating and training users in proper security practises, ensuring that they are aware of the risks they will encounter when using their personal and the organization's systems. Those who disregard their training or behave maliciously to cause loss of the organization's knowledge (by selling it to a competitor, for example) or to inflict damage or loss as a form of retaliation will be left. However, making users aware of potential dangers, weaknesses, and consequences is an important element of training. There is little the organisation can do to assure that users never make a mistake, while some organisations levy a fine on employees who leave important papers or their computer unattended as a way of decreasing the risk. Implementing very strict access control mechanisms and introducing monitoring software that looks for anomalies in user behaviour and flags up an early warning if something out of character is detected can help prevent or reduce the likelihood of information theft or damage to systems and information to some extent. As a form of early identification of fraud, banks and credit card firms take a similar strategy, and will frequently call a customer if they appear to be making transactions that do not fit previous spending patterns.

Users gain awareness by receiving the knowledge they require to avoid making mistakes. Individuals and organisation users who are aware of cyber security issues can function as a first – or even last – line of defence in the fight against cyber-attacks. It should never be thought of as a one-time activity, but rather as an ongoing aspect of human growth that is less formal than training.

People can learn about the hazards they confront every time they use a computer, the strategies employed by social engineers to achieve their aims, the vulnerabilities they or their organisation face, and finally the potential consequences of their actions or inactions through an awareness programme. This doesn't mean that everyone needs to be a cyber security expert; rather, a basic level of understanding is required, similar to how we need to know how to operate the vehicle, the rules of the road, and the dangers we face when driving a car, but we don't need to know how the engine management system works.

There are several steps to developing an awareness programme, just like any other procedure. The programme is planned and designed first. Here, we must choose the most appropriate themes for awareness, such as email etiquette, proper information asset management, and password security, among others. Then we need to establish a business case to justify any cost and a way to communicate with the users. Following that, we may deploy and maintain the programme by creating materials and content as well as launching an awareness campaign. We should set aside time as we move forward to analyse and change the programme as needed, by assessing the campaign's effectiveness and refining and updating the material with new information. Because new individuals will join the organisation and need to be included in the programme, and new threats and vulnerabilities will emerge, awareness is a journey, not a destination. The campaign should emphasise constant reinforcement through methods such as poster campaigns and pop-ups when consumers log on to the internet.

Initial communication with the user community should include informing them that something will be happening in which they will need to participate, as well as offering a rough understanding of what the programme would include, so that their expectations may be handled. We need to provide people a better grasp of the programme so that they comprehend the ramifications for them. We must ensure timely involvement so that people understand that a new method of working exists, as well as user acceptance so that the user community begins to work in the new way. We need to ensure that people are fully committed to new ways of working so that they do not resort to old habits. The security staff should act as evangelists, encouraging others to follow in their footsteps.

Any public awareness campaign will meet obstacles. It's easy to believe that once an awareness campaign is launched, everything will go according to plan, and organisations will only have to react and respond to problems as they happen. However, if organisations are alerted about some of the potential concerns, they should have a contingency plan in place so that they can react more quickly. One of the first challenges is a lack of comprehension. When the awareness campaign begins, it is critical that the message sent to the target audience communicates not just what the organisation hopes to accomplish, but also why it is doing so. This will help the initiative gain a lot of traction. Another stumbling block is the introduction of new technology, which confuses an already complicated programme. Such changes in an organization's IT infrastructure can either improve or complicate the ability to deliver the message; however, as long as people from that part of the organisation are included in the awareness programme, the team should be aware of the possibility before it occurs and be able to incorporate it into their programme or work around the problem. Another stumbling block is using a "one-size-fits-all" strategy, which will not work for everyone. Every organisation is unique, and there are no standard ways for implementing an awareness campaign, and even within a single organisation, different audiences may have different needs. In addition, the scale and scope of an awareness programme for a large organisation and one for a small business will differ significantly. Attempting to offer too much information creates further challenges. Because many users in an organisation are non-technical, the program's focus must accommodate for the fact that the more technical components of cyber security may overwhelm them. It's critical to keep the focus on what the audience needs to know rather than trying to make the information delivery excessively technical. Less is more in this case. Difficulties may occur in the program's continuing management. If this happens, the programme is likely to fail due to a lack of support from the areas of the organisation involved in its implementation, thus senior management engagement is required. Failure to follow up is also a problem. These can and will pose issues for the programme, as it is critical for the team to know how well the message was heard, understood, and acted upon by the intended audience. The delivery of a high-quality programme necessitates regular monitoring and assessments. Inappropriate targeting of the subject matter poses a more nuanced difficulty. This can have a detrimental influence on the programme, because certain groups within the organisation may get awareness material that has little or no impact on their roles, while others may not receive information that is critical to their daily operations. As a result, a tailored strategy is extremely beneficial, but it comes at a cost. Inherited behaviour is a major roadblock. In a programme like this, this is a perpetual struggle. 'We've always done it this way and it's worked, so why should we change?' certain people will always question the programme. Any organisation conducting an awareness campaign should anticipate this type of reaction and have solid counterarguments. Some people believe that security is the duty of the information technology department. This misconception must be countered throughout the public awareness effort. Cyber security is a problem that affects everyone in the company and isn't limited to a single business function.

The formation of a small team to develop and execute the programme is the first step in the planning and design process. Some of them will, by definition, have some knowledge of information security, while others may represent portions of the organisation that could be severely harmed in the event of a cyber-attack. Because a programme like this may be audited at a later point, it's always helpful to have audit on your side. It may also be beneficial to involve the internal audit function, who may be able to offer constructive recommendations. The team's first responsibility will be to identify the program's exact aims and objectives, including whether the target audience will be the entire organisation or simply a small portion as a test project. This latter method may be far more advantageous, as it should be able to achieve its goals on a smaller, and hence less expensive, scale than targeting the entire organisation before expanding the programme to encompass everyone. The target audience for the first phase of the programme may be confined to a single type of user, such as employees who work full-time on the company's premises. This is usually the type of person who will gain the most from cyber security awareness training. Home-based users are another option, with similar but significantly more demanding requirements. These users may require a slightly greater level of understanding of the issues at stake due to the varied criteria for connecting to the organization's network. We can also think of third-party users like contractors, outsourced employees, and suppliers who need access to the organization's networks to do their jobs. System administrators and IT support employees are another target group, as they will already be familiar with the concerns. Users at the management level are especially important since they may be accountable for in-house staff or users who work from home, and they must understand how cyber security issues may affect their departments. Senior executive users may also be targeted, as they will be in charge of many of the corporate choices that a successful cyber-attack may have an influence on. Alternatively, the organisation may choose to target a cross-section of users from other categories in order to demonstrate the entire organisational benefits rather than just those for a specific community. Some themes will be more relevant to specific target groups, such as concerns of social engineering, which may be more important to employees who interact with customers and suppliers on a daily basis than those who do not. This isn't to say that folks with less external contact shouldn't be involved in that element of awareness; it just means that they could get less out of it.

The team must then precisely define the subjects that will be discussed in the programme. It is unnecessary to try to cover all aspects of cyber awareness because this will merely overwhelm the audience; instead, the programme should focus on a relatively narrow subset such as usernames and passwords, spam email, or social engineering at first. Once the outcomes of the earlier work have been assessed and the approaches utilised have been refined where necessary, the campaign can be expanded at a later stage. The message will be communicated to the user community in a variety of ways, including posters that can be posted in areas where workers can easily engage with the message, such as conference rooms and other shared areas. Another alternative is to send out newsletters, which can be distributed via desk-drop in office buildings or by email to offices and home workers. We might also think about giving out objects like coasters, coffee mugs, key fobs, and mouse mats, which reinforce the overall message for as long as they are used. Screensavers might show a variety of messages that could be altered at regular intervals or whenever a new message was needed. Intranet websites could offer useful tips, examples of good and bad cyber security behaviour, and links to more information and training. Fact sheets and pamphlets that are applicable to a certain group inside the organisation, the entire organisation, or a specific business sector. Presentations during team meetings in which a guest speaker speaks for a few minutes on a current topic and answers questions about the entire awareness campaign, keeping the presentation 'short and sweet.' Computer-based training (CBT), which provides a more in-depth degree of information, may be a need for some users' jobs. This could involve, for example, data protection legislation. Once this portion of the project is completed, the team may need to contact senior management or the board of directors for financial approval, as it is impractical to expect the work to be completed for free. As with any business cases, the strategy should concentrate on the possible consequences of not proceeding with the job, as well as the benefits that will accrue if it does. Another argument for confining the initial phase of the campaign to a minimal volume of material is that it will save money and make it simpler for the board to approve it. When the programme moves on to cover more aspects of cyber security awareness, success at this early stage will make obtaining board support for additional expenditure much easier. If the costs are split down into manageable sections, such as the hourly costs of workers who will be delivering the awareness campaign as well as those who will be receiving it, the costs may be identified more simply. Development expenditures can include the creation and maintenance of any intranet websites, as well as the printing of items like posters and newsletters. Promotional charges, such as branded pens, coffee mugs, key fobs, mouse pads, and other giveaway products, might be examined. External trainers are brought in to deliver all or part of the awareness campaign, which increases training costs. Some will be one-time expenses, while others will be ongoing, and the board will require these to be clearly defined. It should also be able to attempt to estimate the prospective impacts, as directors of organisations will want to know if the programme is cost-effective. Potential consequences can include not only the direct financial losses that can be expected if a specific incident occurs, such as lost sales revenue and the costs of responding to and recovering from the incident, but also indirect losses such as share value, brand, and the organization's reputation, though these can be more subjective in nature.

The campaign's delivery and management are crucial. The target audience is only made aware of what they should know and when they are likely to need the information during the awareness stage. For those organisations with more sophisticated resources, this can be given in a variety of forms, including printed materials, email, electronic newsletters, and intranet portals. The campaign then progresses to the next level, so that the target audience understands why they need to engage and how they may do so effectively. This could include bringing up subjects of awareness at team meetings and giving particular presentations on the subject.

The campaign's evaluation is crucial. We need to see outcomes from previous efforts to assess its effectiveness, and as the campaign grows and expands, the organisation expects to see rewards in the form of fewer or no successful cyber-attacks.

The team must make sure that the entire exercise is meticulously documented, and that at the end of the pilot project, they can demonstrate the benefits so that more of the organisation and additional areas of cyber security awareness may be addressed. Success should spawn success once presented to the board, and the team should be in a stronger position to move on to raise awareness for the organisation as a whole or for specific topics. The presentation should emphasise both financial and non-financial benefits, as well as the value to the company and its external stakeholders, such as suppliers and customers, as well as the sector regulator if applicable, and be completely transparent about both the overall costs and the potential consequences of not proceeding with a full rollout. After the board has committed to this, the pilot user group should be recognised for their contributions, as this will not only emphasise the program's relevance, but will also encourage others to get involved.

Training is a separate topic to think about. While awareness raises knowledge of cyber security risks within an organization's user base, training provides very precise and often highly targeted information to those individuals or groups who have a special need for it. Training, particularly highly technical training, can be costly, but it has a clear payoff in terms of minimising the number of events and the possible financial impact on the organisation, just as awareness does. This can include general training that explains the fundamental concepts of cyber security and provides a solid understanding of the issues. Managers in charge of specialised security design and operational staff may require this. Specialized cyber security training is also available, in which very particular skills are given to a small group of people, such as security personnel who control the organization's security architecture. When it comes to product or technology-specific training, it's important to remember that technology evolves at a breakneck pace, necessitating the need for new courses as time goes on. When establishing business cases, the need for recurring budget allocations for this should be reflected into the cost estimates. Identifying those employees who already have training abilities and can pass on their knowledge to others is one way to cut training expenditures. When budgets are tight, this 'train the trainer' strategy can be effective. The business justifications for both generic and specialised cyber security training will need to be established and presented on a case-by-case basis, and they should be presented in the same way as the awareness programme. Instead of focusing exclusively on the organization's overall benefits by targeting all users inside the organisation, these business cases should additionally address the specialised training needs of individual specialists.

Human Factors

To make an error is part of being human, yet forgiveness may be difficult when an error costs millions of dollars in fines, reputational damage, or competitive disadvantage. Attackers have increasingly recognised and profited from human intrinsic tendency to make mistakes by constantly exploiting the human asset, which is a significant weakness of organisations. Data breaches are frequently caused by phishing, stolen credentials, human error, and privilege misuse. Human mistake is the most common source of a breach, whereas malware-related breaches have continuously reduced. This indicates that attackers no longer need to rely on malware to obtain and keep a foothold in organisations because user exploitation tactics have proven to be so successful. In the United Kingdom, the Information Commissioner's Office (ICO) frequently reports that human error is to blame for the vast majority of data breaches.

Humans in an organisation are a large assault surface that is vulnerable. To protect against malware infiltration and exploitation, firewalls, endpoint detection and response (EDR) technologies, and other security solutions are constantly improving their defences. However, unlike tools that are programmed with inbuilt rules to detect and prevent attacks, preventing employees from clicking on a phishing link that leads to a ransomware attack or from uploading sensitive data to an unauthorised external file share is a much more difficult task for an organisation. Humans lack the programming necessary to detect exploitation attempts. Even if they are aware of what to look out for or what actions to avoid, employees are prone to making rash, irrational decisions based on their current mood. Attackers, vendors, and organisations have all reacted differently to this fact.

As a result of the awareness that humans possess the privileges, accesses, and keys to systems, data, and information of interest, attackers have increased credential theft attempts, phishing assaults, and social engineering attacks. And not everyone is a cybersecurity professional who prioritises adherence to cybersecurity best practises. Employees are rarely aware of the warning signals of being exploited or that certain of their behaviours put the company at danger of a cyber breach. An administrative assistant in a hospital, a bank clerk, a travelling salesperson, a research assistant, or a software engineer developing an application are examples of normal personnel going about their daily tasks. In most companies, less than one in every 100 employees is likely to be a cyber defender or have the cyber awareness and experience to avoid attackers' traps. As a result, if the vast majority of employees in an organisation are vulnerable to being abused and present the easiest link to breach, it's understandable why cybercriminals pursue them with vigour.

Security firms have responded by releasing a slew of new technologies. The creation of user-centric solutions such as user behaviour analytics resulted from seeing users as an exploitation vector (UBA). Existing goods have gained user context thanks to traditional security methods. Phishing simulators, nano-learning cyber modules, gamified cyber ranges, and other security awareness products were created to make employees more cybersecurity aware.

People, processes, and products are typically bolstered as a first line of defence for businesses. To make employees more security conscious, organisations invest in new security solutions, create new security policies and procedures, and enforce periodic security awareness training. Despite this, we hear about a ransomware attack, a data breach, an insider information leak, or some other type of compromise every other day or so. Why is this the case, and can it be improved? To further understand this, we looked at the challenges of current ways to dealing with the human attack surface and, as a result, the risk.

When it comes to dealing with the human attack surface, we confront a number of obstacles, including:

1. Daily decisions that are critical, complex and compete with each other

Employees are faced with a variety of daily decisions that affect the security posture of an organisation. To meet corporate objectives, the average employee uses email, file sharing programmes, and external devices to handle business-sensitive and non-sensitive information, with cyber security safeguards not being top of mind. Employees are also routinely targeted by phishing scams, are forced to visit a variety of risky websites, download software to make their duties simpler, and hundreds of other scenarios. These choices result in the organisation being either protected or exposed to security threats. Employees, on the other hand, are rarely aware of the best decision to make, especially when they need it the most.

2. Changing one's behaviour is difficult.

Organizations provide security awareness training to employees or invest in tools like phishing simulators that teach employees about proper cyber hygiene, acceptable use regulations, and compliance mandates to lessen the vulnerability individuals pose. Unfortunately, this does not always result in the expected results. Although most people are aware that using the same password on several accounts is a security issue, a considerable percentage still do so, demonstrating that awareness does not always equate to action. This is largely due to the difficulty of modifying one's behaviour. Building excellent cyber and compliance hygiene needs constant enforcement and discipline, just like any other healthy habit. Many security awareness systems include online learning sessions, quizzes, or even emailing a report of infractions to provide feedback to users and let them know how they're doing on their current "hygiene score." This isn't a full-fledged answer. While training and awareness are at the forefront of the mind throughout the training, they rapidly fade into the background when the day-to-day grind begins. While some security awareness tools track the number of cyber hygiene infractions and send the information straight to the employee through email, the employee doesn't see it until they read their emails, which is often after the issue has occurred. While this form of feedback method is a step in the right direction, it is not supplied at the time when the employee is most susceptible to influence–during the incident.

3.   Inconsistent security tools

Security awareness software is often used in isolation from other software. While some data loss prevention (DLP) technologies contain messaging features to warn employees about non-compliance while handling sensitive data, the tools rarely advise users about improper cyber hygiene practises, such as visiting a dangerous site or falling victim to a phishing effort. Employee feedback is not often provided by EDR tools, email security appliances, or web filtering tools. As a result, while all of these techniques are beneficial, they do not entirely address the issues at hand.

4.   Human risk lurking in plain sight

Human risk is rarely considered in cyber posture evaluations. The evaluations seek for misconfigured services or systems that haven't been patched. As a result, CISOs lack security event data, rarely give a complete context of the user and their behaviours, and rarely communicate with employees in real time to mitigate the risk they provide across multiple dimensions. This context can be extremely useful to an organisation, for example, does a user with poor cyber hygiene or a low compliance score constitute a higher danger to the company? The answer is most likely yes. Analysts should keep this in mind at the very least while triaging occurrences.

It is obvious from this that Cyber, and Information Security is sometimes treated from a technology-centric perspective, in which the human components of sociotechnical systems are viewed as their weakest link, with little regard for end users' cognitive qualities, demands, and motivations. A more holistic Human Factors (HF) approach is required, in which organisations analyse people, organisational, and technology factors in order to demonstrate how HF vulnerabilities may impact cybersecurity risks.

We must do a top–down and bottom–up analysis of our organisation in order to determine its level of maturity in terms of its ability to face and respond to cyber threats and attacks. This method takes a user-centred approach, incorporating both management and staff in the process. Better cyber-security culture isn't necessarily accompanied by more rule-abiding behaviour. Human Factors may be triggered by conflicts between cybersecurity standards and practises. Finally, combining standard technological solutions with guidelines to improve infosec systems through the use of HF in cybersecurity may lead to the adoption of non-technical countermeasures (such as user awareness) for a full and holistic approach to managing cyber security in organisations.

Technical and social vulnerabilities are primarily caused or contributed to by human and organisational factors. Business transformation has resulted in an increase in the number of smart people, their delocalization, and the resulting modification of an organization's defence perimeter; changes in supply-chain dynamics, such as supply predictions and provisioning chains, as well as changes in working habits. Changes in business, travel, and supplying habits have reduced supply chains (i.e., fewer parties involved and a smaller geographic spread) while also making them more robust (e.g., based mostly on trusted and resilient relationships) and less susceptible to external disturbances (e.g., lockdowns). This unusual set-up has bred cyber-crime in a number of weakly secured and vulnerable sectors. Human Factor (HF) vulnerabilities are among the most commonly targeted types of attacks. Online fraud, DDoS (Distributed Denial of Service), drive-by download, and social engineering attacks are only a few examples. Social engineering assaults, in particular, are among the top risks because they target the 'people link,' tricking them into exposing secret information or rendering sophisticated security mechanisms useless through influence and persuasion.

Information Security has been studied as a complicated socio-technical system in which several components interact with legitimate users to maintain the system secure. Organizational, technological, and environmental issues are all possible components. Humans continue to be a key component of an organization's cyber defence, as they are critical variables in the success or failure of information security.

We can deconstruct Human Factors and claim that the first barrier we must overcome is of individuality. Errors and/or violations are both examples of incorrect security activities. Only a few have malicious intent (e.g., acts of sabotage), whereas the majority are the result of improper work element configurations, resulting in unintentional and non-deliberate violations, as well as deliberate non-malicious intent activities. Individual variability related to the likelihood of error-producing situations and violations can be analysed using a variety of psychological frameworks. We can look into consolidated models that use the mediating impact of behavioural intention to link behaviours and attitudes. Employee attitudes toward cybersecurity-critical behaviours can be used to explain human errors and violations. Because cybersecurity may be improved, attitudes predict actual behavioural intentions of risky behaviours in a straightforward way. Because cybersecurity can be improved by pushing a specific set of individual factors that can shape attitudes, such as subjective norms; beliefs in the perceived consequences of an action; actual knowledge of the cybersecurity topic; the preferred cognitive strategies used in a decision-making process, etc., attitudes represent a crucial factor in avoiding security breaches related to deliberate actions determining an unwanted violation of a security rule. Employee attitudes can also enable the influence of more social and organisational factors such as social norms, ethical dilemmas, and different levels of behavioural control perceived by the employee (i.e., the degree of freedom perceived to enact a given behaviour and the contextual barriers/enablers in place, related to such a given behaviour). When it comes to defining security breaches as violations, other psychological frameworks might be used, emphasising the significance of norms and ethical principles in developing employee attitudes. The levels of moral duty and the explicit awareness of the consequences of a given behaviour can both alter attitudes. Employees who are well-informed and trained reduce the number of unintentional and non-deliberate activities that result in a breach of cybersecurity laws, and they play an important role in reducing information security risks. Understanding the complexities of human errors and violations can assist in identifying the areas that have the most impact on overall system security.

The second barrier to overcome is one of organisational context. Employees are guided by explicit policies, methods, and procedures to maintain the system secure. Employees are expected to be compliant by their employers. Formal methods, on the other hand, do not govern human behaviour. Indeed, humans can configure and utilise a system in unanticipated and/or unprotected modes, as well as take shortcuts in the sake of efficiency or simply being helpful, even if it means committing a violation. The motive for deviating from recommended practise may be founded on informal procedures and intuitive cost–benefit analyses, in which the predicted benefits outweigh the potential negative implications of one's actions. As a result, when organisational policies and procedures are regarded too costly, or when employees are unsure how to put them into practise in real-life situations, they are simply ignored. Procedures should be viewed as tools for action rather than as a prediction of human behaviour. Procedures must be comprehended; their effectiveness is dependent on the knowledge required rather than mindless acceptance. Improved Infosec communication is a challenge for businesses looking to avoid security breaches. Some consumers regard information security as a technological discipline handled solely by security specialists, claiming that IT has failed to communicate with end users about proper security practises. When the security function distributes guidance to users, they frequently complain about a lack of time to read it, a lack of communication about where the documentation is located, a lack of incentives for studying the documentation, and a lack of knowledge to understand security management instructions. Users will be more motivated to seek security information on their own if there is effective communication. Building an information security culture that embeds information security across the organisation requires a renewed focus on behavioural challenges. Indeed, a strong information security culture can help to reduce the risk posed by employee behaviour when it comes to dealing with and processing data. An organization's security culture shows how management approaches and responds to security issues. Security efficacy is determined by a successful security governance programme, the quality of senior management support, continuous reviews, and the implementation of adjustments to meet new challenges. All of these factors are influenced by the organisational culture, as well as the top management's interest and attention, as they have the ability to influence HF-related cyber threats and attacks.

The third barrier to overcome is one of technology. Although security must be user-centric, most organisations are still grappling with how to apply user-experience principles to increase usability. In the domain of cybersecurity, poor usability usually leads to ineffective deployment of cybersecurity technologies and capabilities, reducing their efficacy. Some in the IT industry believe that cybersecurity is a barrier to usability, especially when it comes to keeping data, systems, and devices secure for vulnerable groups. When employing usable security design heuristics, there are challenges with considering person differences and other socio-cultural aspects. Adaptive and/or personalised user interfaces have been proposed as possible solutions to usability and acceptability concerns in various user domains and circumstances. Positive attitudes toward the proper usage of software and procedures will result from improvements in interface design and user experience. User-centric security products, services, and policies should adhere to HCI principles and be tailored to the needs of a specific organization's users in order to improve users' understanding of information security.

The fourth barrier to overcome is one of ethics. Organizational transformation can be extremely useful, but it can also raise ethical concerns, such as increased information sharing. In healthcare, for example, information databases have improved communication between organisations and practitioners, but they have also raised concerns about the relationship between patients, healthcare providers, and professionals, as well as how confidentiality, integrity, and availability are safeguarded. Information security, with a focus on data protection and technology protection, has complex interrelationships in facilitating or hindering what health technology aims to achieve (i.e., quality and efficiency of services; privacy; usability; and safety) and medical ethics principles (i.e. respect for autonomy, for patients' rights to decide for themselves about medical treatments; non-maleficence, to reduce risks for patients resulting from medical actions/interactions). These are the tensions that arise when critical data in emergency situations (e.g., when the patient is no longer able to agree on data accessibility, and/or when sharing the patient's data among healthcare professionals to improve the quality and efficiency of treatment) is not accessible to ensure a patient's privacy and autonomy (i.e., patient password protection and encryption). As a result, when ethical elements are challenged by individual or group ideas, personal moral ideals, and behaviours, individuals may suffer ethical dissonances in many corporate contexts and scenarios (e.g., in human–machine interactions).

There is a way by which we can go about analysing all of these distinct issues that are at play. It is necessary to take a holistic approach. We can use the Human Aspects of Information Security Questionnaire (HAIS – Q) to analyse interactions and vulnerabilities at the person level. The HAIS–Q questionnaire is based on the idea that as computer users' knowledge of cybersecurity policy and procedures grows, so does their attitude and belief in information security policy and processes, leading to more risk-averse information security behaviour. Employee "Knowledge" (K) about policy and procedures, "Attitudes" (A) toward policy and procedures, and self-reported "Behaviours" (B) are investigated in the Knowledge-Attitude-Behaviour (KAB) model (B). The HAIS-Q allows researchers to investigate the KAB model using seven user scenarios, dubbed "focal areas" (FAs): (FA1) password management, (FA2) e-mail use, (FA3) internet use, (FA4) mobile computing, (FA5) social networking, (FA6) incident reporting, and (FA7) information processing. These seven FAs cover all security policy information that is relevant to employers and computer users who are most likely to break the rules. The HAIS-Q questionnaire contains 63 items on a 5-point Likert scale (1 = Strongly Agree, 5 = Strongly Disagree), divided into three batteries of items corresponding to the KAB components: the first battery contains 21 items measuring employees' "Knowledge," the second battery contains 21 items measuring employees' "Attitude," and the third battery contains 21 items measuring employee self-reported "Behavior." Each of the battery's 21 items covers three themes for each of the seven FAs, allowing the investigation of the same FA to progress through the KAB components (i.e., asking three questions about the "Knowledge," then the "Attitude," and finally the employee's actual "Behaviour" on that FA). The elements might be given in random order and not clustered according to the KAB model to avoid bias and minimise any sequencing effect. As a result, we may compare the scores obtained by items belonging to the same FA, as well as the cases in which KAB components had a direct or indirect link. After that, the responses can be analysed.

To assess organisational context, we can use focus groups and semi-structured interviews to help us understand how organisational characteristics may influence employees' risk-related behaviours. The goal of focus groups is to have a better understanding of the findings that emerge from the HAIS-Q questionnaire replies. They only require a small sample of volunteers from the questionnaire responses. Participants can be chosen in a way that reflects the diversity of professional vocations. Sessions may take up to 1.5 hours. Top managers should not be included because they can be recruited for semi-structured interviews. Topics/security scenarios produced from the FAs of the HAIS-Q questionnaire and the taxonomy of human errors and violations framework can be included in the focus group guideline. Semi-structured interviews are used to collect managers' and employee representatives' perspectives on the organization's information security challenges. They are used to learn how people make security decisions, how they assess risk and evaluate security-critical situations, and what the most common cybersecurity policy violations are. Interviews with a variety of managers and employee representatives are possible. Chief Executive Officers (CEOs), Chief Financial Officers (CFOs), Chief Information Security Officers (CISOs), and other staff representatives, such as IT experts and operational positions, are typical examples. The 45-minute semi-structured interviews can include cybersecurity themes derived from the Cybersecurity Maturity model, such as governance and people, policy and processes, operations, technical controls, and attack response.

Every organisation should focus on the operator-specific needs and constraints of the work activity to reduce the opportunities for conflicts between security and work efficiency objectives, in order to understand human vulnerabilities and the reason for incorrect security actions taking the form of both errors and violations.

Non-technical countermeasures can be used to enhance an organization's human factor and help it become more effective in the face of cyber-attacks and threats. To promote and implement usable rules and practises, as well as nurture accountability and the circulation of critical/relevant information, the author recommends using an interwoven and user-centred design approach. The following procedures should be done to create a macro-ergonomic framework, which is regarded a critical aspect in successful cybersecurity management:

- Demonstrate leadership that emphasises the importance of security. If executives do not take cybersecurity risks seriously, neither will their company or their employees.

- Hold everyone accountable for their security responsibilities. From the CEO on down, everyone should be responsible for ensuring that their reports adhere to appropriate cyber hygiene.

- Assess the risk perception of employees while creating the material of information security awareness programmes to mitigate the apparent benefits they may foresee in unsafe behaviours. Even when understanding of security provisions is adequate and behaviour appears to be in line with them, the perception of risks and benefits has an impact on attitudes toward security policies and procedures.

- Enhance the usability of technologies that support work-related tasks such as job coordination and information exchange, while ensuring that security constraints do not detract from the user experience. The danger of inappropriate usage of personal devices and applications with lower levels of security is reduced when the user experience is satisfactory. Improvements in Human Computer Interaction (HCI) - specifically interface design and UX interaction - will have a positive impact on the overall information security socio-technical system because they reduce actual misuse of technical tools like software or procedures and improve positive attitudes toward their proper use. User-centric security product, service, and policy design should adhere to HCI principles, and products tailored to the specific needs of a specific organisation in a specific setting improve users' understanding of information security.

- Use a customised approach when creating security policies and training programmes so that security awareness messages are tailored to the employees' knowledge and skills and targeted to specific information security areas. Consider the differences between IT and non-IT employees, as well as the distinction between well-established Focus Areas like Password Management and less well-established ones like Social Networking.

- Create a culture that is safe and just. This is how can managers demonstrate the importance of cybersecurity throughout the organisation. Their actions must not contradict security policies. When it comes to common cybersecurity perceptions, deeds speak louder than words. We need to get rid of the fear of honesty and make the repercussions of lying more severe. Managers must walk the walk and not just talk the talk when it comes to cybersecurity. They must recognise and reward good cybersecurity behaviour while punishing bad behaviour. If all we speak about is efficiency and performance, we're delivering the idea that security isn't as critical. Encourage employees to report security-related issues without fear of being blamed for non-malicious violations in a safe and just culture setting.

- Increase user motivation and knowledge, fostering an atmosphere in which people participate actively in the improvement of security measures and are encouraged to provide constructive feedback on their potential limits.

- Establish explicit guidelines for sharing information. When determining the scope of corporate information that people can communicate in the course of their work and what breaches business confidentiality boundaries, CISOs have difficult considerations. The rise of social media and data protection legislation is becoming increasingly significant. Efforts to solve this issue, however, should not obstruct lawful information sharing. If the methods for sharing information with third parties are unclear or unworkable, employees may be enticed to find other ways to share it, leaving it open to attackers if it escapes the company's control.

- Be aware of your physical security. While many cybersecurity measures focus on technology as both a source and a remedy for cyber threats, the physical element should never be overlooked when assessing human factor concerns. Common courtesy, a lack of security awareness, and a reluctance to question non-employees about their presence amplify the problem. Outsiders are allowed to tailgate into offices because people hold open doors. If employees are used to seeing strangers strolling around their workplace, they are less likely to confront them, but it could be someone who has gotten unauthorised access. As a result, we require an effective visitor control policy.

- Make certain that workloads do not jeopardise security. Workloads that are unreasonable are not only bad practise; they are also a danger issue. When people are overworked, they are more likely to make mistakes. Filling their workday with email traffic can help them achieve this. It's more difficult to notice a phishing email if you're dealing with emails in a rush and not paying attention to them correctly.

- Look for ways to protect your identity other than passwords. Passwords should be phased out completely. Many of us would agree with this view from a convenience standpoint, but there is also a security case for using different methods of identity verification. Passwords are such a weak spot. Business leaders must invest in facial, palm-vein, and fingerprint identification technologies in order to eliminate our reliance on passwords.

- Make staff aware of the threat's magnitude. Employees must be aware of the actual threats that their company has faced, whether or not the attack was successful. Although it may seem counterintuitive to emphasise the financial consequences of security breaches, it is critical for employees to understand the scope and severity of real and potential crises. Real-life examples should be used in cybersecurity training. People must believe that this isn't just something that happens to others.

- Cybersecurity training cannot be viewed as a one-time checkbox exercise. Part of managing risk is ensuring that staff knowledge is up to date. Organizations must know how many people have been trained, to what level of comprehension, and whether or not refresher training is needed to keep employees up to date on incidents, scams, and other issues.

- When developing security policies, consult with employees to confirm the impact of trade-offs between security measures and processes that support other organisational goals, such as work efficiency and safety. Analyse the working environment's opportunities and constraints, as well as the requirements for the most crucial jobs, to ensure that important security barriers are not bypassed only to get the job done. We must strike a balance between the requirement for security and people's ability to execute their jobs. When developing procedures, we consult with employees to better understand how security policies will affect their job.

Printed in Great Britain
by Amazon

17176384R00079